Cambridge Elements ≡

Elements in Politics and Communication
edited by
Stuart Soroka
University of Michigan

HOME STYLE OPINION

How Local Newspapers Can Slow Polarization

Joshua P. Darr
Louisiana State University

Matthew P. Hitt
Colorado State University

Johanna L. Dunaway
Texas A&M University

CAMBRIDGE
UNIVERSITY PRESS

CAMBRIDGE
UNIVERSITY PRESS

University Printing House, Cambridge CB2 8BS, United Kingdom

One Liberty Plaza, 20th Floor, New York, NY 10006, USA

477 Williamstown Road, Port Melbourne, VIC 3207, Australia

314–321, 3rd Floor, Plot 3, Splendor Forum, Jasola District Centre, New Delhi – 110025, India

79 Anson Road, #06–04/06, Singapore 079906

Cambridge University Press is part of the University of Cambridge.

It furthers the University's mission by disseminating knowledge in the pursuit of education, learning, and research at the highest international levels of excellence.

www.cambridge.org
Information on this title: www.cambridge.org/9781108948098
DOI: 10.1017/9781108950930

First published 2021

A catalogue record for this publication is available from the British Library.

ISBN 978-1-108-94809-8 Paperback
ISSN 2633-9897 (online)
ISSN 2633-9889 (print)

Home Style Opinion

How Local Newspapers Can Slow Polarization

Elements in Politics and Communication

DOI: 10.1017/9781108950930
First published online: March 2021

Joshua P. Darr
Louisiana State University

Matthew P. Hitt
Colorado State University

Johanna L. Dunaway
Texas A&M University

Author for correspondence: Joshua P. Darr, jdarr@lsu.edu

Abstract: Local newspapers can hold back the rising tide of political division in America by turning away from the partisan battles in Washington and focusing their opinion page on local issues. When a local newspaper in California dropped national politics from its opinion page, the resulting space filled with local writers and issues. We use a preregistered analysis plan to show that after this quasi-experiment, politically engaged people did not feel as far apart from members of the opposing party, compared to those in a similar community whose newspaper did not change. While it may not cure all of the imbalances and inequities in opinion journalism, an opinion page that ignores national politics could help local newspapers push back against political polarization.

Keywords: local news, polarization, opinion journalism, newspaper, experiment

ISBNs: 9781108948098 (PB), 9781108950930 (OC)
ISSNs: 2633-9897 (online), 2633-9889 (print)

Contents

1 What We Did on Our Summer Vacation

Sudden extensions in communication are reflected in cultural disturbances.
– Harold Innis, 1951

On June 8, 2019, Google alerted us that our research was mentioned in a California newspaper. We are always pleasantly surprised when our work is noticed, but this was more than a passing reference. In her column, Julie Makinen, Executive Editor of *The Desert Sun*, the English-language daily newspaper based in Palm Springs, announced a plan to drop national politics from her newspaper's opinion page for the month of July. Her plan was inspired by our findings that local newspapers can hold back the forces of polarization (Darr, Hitt, and Dunaway 2018). She was motivated by a similar question: "In an era where there seem to be countless forums for people to scream about national politics, are we devoting the right amount of space to local and state issues?" (Makinen 2019a).

In the dwindling yet durable local newspaper industry, editors, reporters, and owners are grappling with changing economics, technological upheaval, and where to focus their attention. Local journalism monitors local institutions for corruption (Rubado and Jennings 2019), provides a community public forum (Hindman 2014; Mondak 1995), and highlights positive stories about the community (Rosen 1993), but increasingly lacks the resources to meet critical community information needs (Friedland et al. 2012). Modern media technologies liberate media and consumers from geographic constraints (Abramson, Arterton, and Orren 1988), allowing audience migration to the detriment of local news. In many communities, national news fills the void. Americans want news about the president and Congress and have nearly unlimited options to find it online, in print, and on television (Hopkins 2018).

The Desert Sun took a stand against the creeping nationalization of American political news by refocusing its opinion page on local authors and issues. Makinen decided the newspaper would take a "month long summer holiday in July from national politics on *The Desert Sun*'s Opinion pages . . . no columns, no cartoons and no letters about the [P]resident, Congress, the Supreme Court, etc." (Makinen 2019a).

Like most months of Donald Trump's presidency, July 2019 experienced a fever pitch of heavily reported partisan conflict. Former FBI Director, Robert Mueller, testified before Congress on July 24 about his report on potential collusion between Trump's presidential campaign and Russia. The month was bookended by Democratic presidential primary debates, on June 26 and 27 and July 30 and 31. On July 17, a crowd at a Trump rally in Greenville, North Carolina, chanted "Send her back!" at Trump's mention of Representative Ilhan Omar, the Democrat representing Minnesota's fifth congressional district (McCarthy 2019). There was no shortage of national politics news in July 2019, but it was missing from the opinion page of *The Desert Sun*.

We immediately recognized the opportunity to learn from this experiment. We fielded surveys in June and July to assess political attitudes before and after the localization experiment, targeting respondents in the circulation ZIP codes of *The Desert Sun* and a comparison newspaper that did not change its opinion page, the *Ventura County Star*. We were particularly interested in the impact of localizing the opinion page on affective and social polarization. Defined as dislike and distrust of the opposing party and measured using opinions of politicians, opposing partisans, and increased social distance between partisans, affective polarization is to blame for many problems in American politics today, from legislative gridlock to partisan differences in mask-wearing during the COVID-19 pandemic (Igielnik 2020; Iyengar et al. 2019; Mason 2018). When the news substitutes "an intense focus on the partisan war in Washington" (Makinen 2019a) for stories that emphasize membership in one's geographic community, priming these cross-cutting identities may cool tensions and dampen anger (Mason 2016).

We conducted a complete content analysis of *The Desert Sun*'s opinion page in June, July, and August 2019 and found that the newspaper followed through on their commitment: mentions of President Donald Trump fell to nearly zero, total syndicated content dropped by half, and local issues such as downtown development, traffic congestion, architectural restoration, and environmental concerns received more attention. Localization did not make the opinion page resemble the community, however: July amplified the voices of prototypical political elites rather than women and racial and ethnic minorities. Reflecting newspapers' longstanding tendency to cater to elites, diversity on the opinion page often means representing ideas from both the right and left, not diversity among the authors (Abramson et al. 1988).

The local-only opinion page slowed polarization for readers of *The Desert Sun* relative to readers of the *Ventura County Star* on both affective and social dimensions, consistent with recent studies showing that op-eds can durably change attitudes (Coppock et al. 2018). These effects are moderated by political interest, knowledge, and preference for local news: political sophisticates are less polarized by local than national opinion content. Sadly, local newspapers are shrinking, disappearing, or becoming "ghosts" of their former selves that merely host syndicated content (Abernathy 2018). Philanthropists, newspaper owners, and editors can reduce affective polarization by supporting dedicated opinion editors focused on the community and what it needs to know.

Using a design with high external validity and causal leverage, we show that local newspapers can slow the rise of affective and social polarization through a refocusing of their opinion pages on local issues. When national politics was eliminated, local voices and state-level concerns filled the gap. Our findings demonstrate the continued importance of local opinion pages, which are receiving less support from newspaper chain owners and professional associations (Enda 2013). We hope that the news industry and philanthropists take these findings as a reason to reinvest in local opinion journalism.

1.1 Home Style Opinion

Cultivating a local audience is a well-established political and media strategy. In his 1978 book, *Home Style: Representatives in Their Districts*, political scientist Richard Fenno described how members of Congress historically adopted a "home style" to gain the trust of their constituencies to win reelection. Congressional home styles imbued everything a representative did, from the clothes they wore to the votes they cast, showing voters that their representative was "one of them." For decades, this strategy paid electoral dividends. Voters consistently reported liking their representative but disliking Congress overall (Fenno 1978). But for today's elected officials, crafting a home style may be less useful as national parties and politics increasingly dictate representatives' behavior in Congress (Quinn 2020; Kujala 2019; Hetherington 2001). The reelection prospects of today's representatives may not be as dependent on strong and consistent local identities (Trussler 2020).

The weaker ties and lower responsiveness between House representatives and their local constituents resembles a similar pattern in local media. As audiences turn away from local news in favor of national news, members of the House have less incentive to attend the geographic constituency as district service goes largely unnoticed and fails to generate electoral rewards without attention from the local press (Trussler 2020). In spite of the fact that local media are still more trusted than national media (Guess, Nyhan and Reifler 2018), evolutions in communication technologies chipped away at the geographic boundaries constraining market audiences and eroded these safeguards of electoral accountability. At the same time, for the remaining local media, a local focus is still a safe bet. Local news outlets need a home style, since audiences trust and follow local media because of the local coverage they provide (Knight Foundation 2019).

For those politicians and newspapers trying to appeal to locals, home style comprises both art and substance, adopting and perpetuating regional preferences and norms while contributing to the health and well-being of the region. If a newspaper publishes only wire reports without serving community information needs, readers will turn elsewhere. Newspapers often narrow their appeals in response to economic pressures and audience characteristics (Gentzkow and Shapiro 2010; Branton and Dunaway 2009; Hamilton 2004). The top priority of local newspapers, including on the opinion page, is to provide readers with a local angle (Rosenfeld 2000).

The Desert Sun, 93 years old in 2020, is the area's only English-language daily newspaper, along with just two television news stations. Its home style is both economic and linguistic, distinguishing *The Desert Sun* from an all-Spanish newspaper (*El Informador del Valle*) and a bilingual newspaper (*La Prensa Hispana*) that serve the region's substantial Hispanic and Latinx population. Economic factors also skew coverage toward the wealthy: "[T]he paper has long catered to a more affluent audience and probably left out more economically disadvantaged communities" (Makinen, personal communication, June 18, 2020).

This pattern of market responsiveness is reflected in a lack of diversity on the opinion page, although the paper is far from unique in this regard. Gender and racial inequality characterize most opinion pages: only 15 percent of op-eds in 1992 (Wolf 1995) and 20 percent in 2011 (Yaeger 2012) were written by women, while white writers continue to dominate opinion journalism and Sunday morning talk shows (Powell 2014). Localization may take up resources that might otherwise be used to overcome these biases. Even a well-meaning newspaper like *The Desert Sun* needs resources to represent the racial and economic diversity of their full geographic constituency, and targeted market responsiveness reflects that resources are often scarce, much like for representatives, who rarely focused their efforts on appealing to their entire district (Fenno 1978).

Appealing across demographic groups within the market audience may be difficult, but local newspapers can adopt a home style that reflects the one shared characteristic across groups in the local market audience – by prioritizing state and local issues. By banning national politics, *The Desert Sun* turned the opinion page over to issues facing California and Palm Springs, prioritizing community voices over journalists' perspectives. Readers filled the pages with appeals to save old buildings, descriptions of the area's natural beauty, and exhortations to drive safely, but the writers did not look more like their community: rather, authors on balance remained largely white, male, and relatively privileged. Localization alone could not overcome newspapers' historical legacy as both a product and a platform for elites (Hindman 2009; Prior 2007; Abramson et al 1998; Innis 1951).

While it may not cure all of the imbalances and inequities of the local opinion page, a turn to "home style opinion" could provide a roadmap for other local newspapers to push back against polarization. In a nationalized and partisan era

(Hopkins 2018), newspapers want to strengthen the community connections that make them unique. As more newspapers are bought by nonlocal owners and cut their newsroom staff and opinion page editors, their home style, cultivated over decades, may nevertheless diminish.

1.2 Less Local News, More Polarization

In the research that inspired Makinen's experiment, we studied the effects of local newspaper closures on Americans' voting decisions (Darr, Hitt, and Dunaway 2018). The United States had lost 2,100 newspapers over the past fifteen years, readership and staffing fell by half, and many of the country's 6,700 remaining newspapers are pale reflections of their former selves (Abernathy 2020). Newspapers are the most important source for local stories that are "original, local, and address a critical information need" (Mahone et al. 2019), and we expected a closure to have polarizing effects.

We collected an original national sample of newspaper closures from 2009 to 2012 to examine if areas where a newspaper closed had more split-ticket voting, in which people vote for different parties at different levels of government – for example, Democrat for president and Republican for senator – than areas without a newspaper closure. We matched counties according to race, voting-age population, gender, income, and education, and compared president-Senate split-ticket voting before (2008) and after (2012) a newspaper left a community. We found a 1.9 percent decrease in split-ticket voting in counties that lost a newspaper (Darr, Hitt, and Dunaway 2018). Robustness tests showed that our findings were best explained by increased reliance on partisan cues, not reduced information. In other words: if local news fails, national news replaces it and polarizes voting behavior.

Our findings clearly tapped into something journalists understood and cared about. Our study was covered by the Associated Press, *Washington Post*, and *Journalist's Resource*, and we wrote about it for *The Conversation* and *Scientific American*. Local journalists and newspapers noticed as well: *The Advocate* of Baton Rouge, Louisiana, the *Charleston Gazette-Mail* of West Virginia, and others wrote editorials about the state of local news framed around our findings. In our interview with her, Makinen described why our study resonated:

> Why do we need to run voices from the *Chicago Tribune* or the *Washington Post*? I'm sure there's local stuff that we can get people interested in here . . .
> As I read your article and other articles that talked about the national polarization trickling down into local media, the more I thought I, we, should try something . . . National columnists would write a lot about Trump and the national political divide. And I felt that was adding to people's unhappiness with the paper, whichever side of it you were on . . . If we could put a focus on

local things, people could find some common ground. Writing another column about Trump is not going to bring anyone in the community together.
(Makinen, personal communication, June 18, 2020)

Makinen made clear that national political news is not only a competitor for
local newspapers: it is an active force within them, in wire services and syndicated columns and letters to the editor. Particularly on the opinion page,
publishing more national politics may contribute to the current wave of polarization and nationalization.

1.3 Palm Springs

Makinen's initiative, not a deliberate research design, determined the location
for our experiment. Palm Springs, located in the Coachella Valley east of Los
Angeles, is not a representative American community in terms of gender, race,
or political leanings, and understanding those differences is necessary for
interpreting our conclusions.

In addition to Palm Springs, *The Desert Sun* serves the cities of Desert Hot
Springs, Cathedral City, Rancho Mirage, Palm Desert, Indian Wells, Indio,
La Quinta, and Coachella (CVAG 2015). Palm Springs has a permanent
population of 48,500, swelling to around 75,000 in winter months (City of
Palm Springs 2020; U.S. Census Bureau 2019). The economy depends on
cultural and environmental tourism for its desert beauty, music festivals such
as Coachella and Stagecoach, and distinctive mid-century modern architecture (Visit Palm Springs 2019). Water and natural preservation are perpetual
concerns for tourism and survival (Makinen, personal communication,
June 18, 2020).

Gay and lesbian voters make up more than half the electorate in Palm
Springs, which elected the nation's first all-LGBTQ+ city council in 2018
(Wilson 2019). Palm Springs' population is only 41.9 percent women, and the
city has one of the highest percentages of same-sex households in the nation
(Gates and Ost 2004). Palm Springs is an outlier in its circulation region,
however: Palm Desert, a similar-sized city next to Palm Springs and also served
by *The Desert Sun*, is 51.8 percent female, and Indio (51.3 percent female) and
Cathedral City (49 percent female) are more representative (U.S. Census
Bureau 2019).

Politically, the area is heavily Democratic: across the Coachella Valley,
Hillary Clinton received over 75 percent of the presidential vote in 2016
(Marx 2016), compared to 62 percent statewide. The political composition of
the area can determine the slant of a newspaper (Gentzkow and Shapiro 2010),
but both Makinen and Franco stressed in their interviews that they strive to keep

the opinion page balanced: "I think it's important to take a hard look at the balance of stuff on our pages and not just dismiss all criticism like that of being completely unworthy of attention" (Makinen, personal communication, June 18, 2020). The newspaper actually broke with its Republican-leaning tradition to endorse Hillary Clinton in 2016, its first ever Democratic endorsement (Desert Sun 2016).

Although the location of our study is not representative, *The Desert Sun* is a fairly typical newspaper, and the outcomes of its opinion page experiment are relevant to local media across America.

1.4 Plan of the Element

In the following Sections, we will illustrate why local news matters; explore how *The Desert Sun*'s opinion page content changed in July 2019; analyze our survey results about polarization; and offer suggestions for using these lessons to strengthen local news.

Section 2 explores the diverging trajectories of local and national news. A community with a declining local newspaper will suffer in several ways: national news exposure lowers familiarity with local elections and exposes consumers to more partisan language. National news cannot supply the civic benefits that local news once did.

Section 3 explores how the content of the opinion page of *The Desert Sun* changed in July 2019. Syndicated columns fell by more than half, Trump coverage dropped to nearly zero, and the opinion page published more letters about local issues while national ones evaporated. State-level syndication and local writers replaced national politics, but racial, ethnic, and gender representation did not improve, and the voices of powerful executives and CEOs were amplified.

In Section 4, we analyze our surveys of Palm Springs and Ventura according to our preregistered hypotheses and analysis plan, focusing on affective and social polarization. Affective and social polarization in Palm Springs slowed down after July, when opinion page mentions of both parties fell by half, relative to Ventura. This effect was moderated by three factors: reading the newspaper, political knowledge, and political participation.

Section 5 lays out our recommendations for local news at this precarious time. Both Makinen and Franco said that other newspapers should localize their opinion pages but acknowledge that it takes resources other newspapers may not have. Philanthropists and newspaper chains should hire or retain opinion editors and support state-level news services. When local newspapers give readers home style opinion instead of national partisan conflict, they can hold back the rising tide of polarization.

2 Why Local Newspapers Matter

Local newspapers foster robust political competition, bolster government performance, and increase citizens' satisfaction with local governance. Communities have critical information needs that help members live safely, access opportunities, and participate in civic life, and local media are the best source for that information (Friedland et al. 2012). As local newspapers disappear from communities and create deserts in many Americans' news diets, those critical information needs go unmet and are replaced by polarizing national news.

Local news differs from national news in several important ways, with consequences for American democracy. First, local news outlets are the only outlets willing and able to meet the critical information needs of local communities and empower democratic accountability (Napoli et al. 2017; Waldman 2011; Arnold 2004). Second, local news outlets are more trusted than their national counterparts (Gramlich, 2019; Guess, Nyhan, and Reifler, 2018), giving local news unique influence over their readers' knowledge, attitudes, and behavior. Third, and most important for our purposes, local news chooses what to cover based on relevance to the community rather than partisan conflict. Local news without the spectacle of national party politics could ease the polarization that grips Americans' political attitudes.

The purpose of this Section is to demonstrate why local newspapers matter. We also detail the threats facing local news, describe how these threats contribute to concerning trends in American politics, and show that exposure to national news does not increase local political knowledge and contains more polarizing language. A local newspaper that emphasizes its home style can reach readers and meet their needs better than national news can.

2.1 Local News and Political Accountability

The downsides of losing local newspapers may seem apparent to some, while others may wonder why they should care. After all, newspapers are arguably an elitist and antiquated way to deliver information, and a poor fit with the conveniences of today's digital media environment. Local television news attracts plenty of criticisms too: it is overly focused on traffic, weather, and sports, and barely discusses public affairs. What is it about local news that makes it so unique and so important? Why can't the rising tide of national news lift all boats?

National outlets cannot and do not cover all 535 legislative offices of the United States Congress, much less the fifty state governments or thousands of municipal governments (Arnold 2004). Instead, they focus on the president and national institutions such as Congress, the courts, and federal agencies (Gardner and Sullivan 1999), with a bias toward institutional and elite conflict (York 2013).

Local coverage of elected officials focuses on their geographic constituency (Arnold 2004). State and local politicians use local news to cultivate their "personal vote," touting their service to locals (Trussler 2018; Fenno 1978). Unlike national outlets, local newspapers are interested in elected officials because of their local relevance, not their leadership positions, ideology, or prominence in Congress. Local newspaper coverage of legislators and their accomplishments for their district particularly influence voters in the opposing party (Schaffner 2006), overcoming partisanship and placing district consider- ations at the top of voters' minds (Trussler 2018). By covering legislators' locally relevant activities, local newspapers deemphasize partisanship, inform voters about their representatives' actions for the district, and provide a platform for local issues (Snyder and Stromberg 2010).

There is a strong link between healthy local journalism and accountability in local government. State government is more corrupt when local coverage is worse, such as in states with remote capitals (Campante and Do 2014). Poorly covered representatives exert less effort for their constituencies, are less likely to vote against their party or serve on relevant committees, and bring less funding back home (Snyder and Stromberg 2010).

Citizens' trust in local news (e.g., Gramlich 2019; Prato 1998) makes it uniquely informative about representatives' activities (Fowler 2020; Miller and Krosnick 2000). Citizens' attentiveness, knowledge, and participation are higher in areas with better local coverage (Hopkins 2018; Hayes and Lawless 2015; Gentzkow et al. 2011). Less local coverage makes local elections less competitive, typically to the benefit of incumbents (Rubado and Jennings 2019; Schulhofer-Wohl and Garrido 2013; but see Gentzkow et al. 2011).

In spite of Americans' trust in their local news, it is not without flaws. Newspapers are often geared towards elite audiences and may perpetuate inequalities in political knowledge. The arrival of broadcast television helped remedy some inequalities by expanding the news audience, but is largely considered superficial, fleeting, and uninformative (Prior 2007). As cable expanded the media landscape in the 1970s and 1980s, it increased pressure to focus on profits, affecting the incentives and outputs of news organizations.

Rising corporate media ownership and consolidation brought superficial coverage, fewer locally focused stories, and less diverse viewpoints (Martin and McCrain 2019; Napoli 2003). Types of owner include chains, local, private, nonprofit, and public-shareholder (Dunaway 2013, 2008; Hamilton 2004;

Schaffner and Sellers 2003). Competition and ownership affect staffing, production processes, and the news product itself (Peterson 2020; Martin and McCrain 2019; Usher 2019; Archer and Clinton 2018; Gentzkow and Shapiro 2010; Dunaway 2008; Hamilton 2004).

Companies that oversee large chains invest less in newsrooms and produce more sensational and less local coverage (Dunaway 2013). Similarly, publicly traded companies maximize profit return to shareholders (Hamilton 2004; Baker 2002), and often reduce staffing and other newsroom resources after taking control. Hedge funds, a new and emerging class of owners, are rapidly buying up local newspapers and stripping them for parts (Abernathy 2018). Like publicly traded companies on steroids, hedge-fund owners slash newsroom staffs and reporting resources (Peterson and Dunaway 2020), drastically reducing the amount of political coverage those newspapers provide (Hare and Laforme 2020; Pompeo 2020; Peterson 2019). Hedge-fund owners brazenly shirk the civic mission of newspapers in favor of maximizing profit margins.

Ownership structures affect news outputs. As newsroom staff decreases, so does the amount and quality of coverage (Peterson 2020; Dunaway 2008), making hedge-fund ownership models particularly troubling (Abernathy 2020). Cost-cutting and aggressive profit-seeking commonly result in frivolous, sensational, and negative coverage of politics (Dunaway and Lawrence 2015; Dunaway 2008; Hamilton 2004).

2.2 Consolidation and Localism

Debates about media consolidation raged throughout the broadcast era. Struggles to ensure that news audiences had access to a diversity of local perspectives began well before the current era of declining local news: in the wake of the 1996 Telecommunications Act, corporate media lobbies increased pressure for further easing of cross-ownership restrictions aimed at preventing local information monopolies. Alarm over rising consolidation compelled a media reform movement from citizen groups concerned about the ability of consolidated corporate media to serve the public interest (McChesney 2004). Media deregulation critics argue that "outsourced news" robs local communities of physically present and familiar journalists that provide higher quality local news coverage (Usher 2019; Hood 2007).

Although local media owners may feel more invested in their community (Yan and Napoli 2006; Napoli and Yan 2007), the evidence regarding the effects of chain media ownership on localism is mixed. Chain owners can exploit economies of scale to provide more public affairs coverage among the individual communities they serve (Hamilton 2004), although there is no convincing evidence that they do so (Hood 2007; Wirth and Wollert 1979). Local owners provide better local public affairs programming than "out of market" owners, however, and television stations owned by chains carry fewer hard news stories about their state's senators (Hamilton 2004; Napoli 2003).

Local newspapers continue to conduct most of the newsgathering in American media (Mahone et al. 2019), even as print media have suffered the most in the age of digital media. Figure 1 depicts newspaper closures occurring between 2000 and 2014, based on our own research (Darr, Hitt, and Dunaway 2018). Each dot represents one daily or weekly newspaper that ceased to exist during that time.

Circulation and revenues continue to decline, and newspapers' web traffic has plateaued. Between 2000 and 2018, weekday newspaper circulation dropped from 56 million American households to 28.3 million, with a 12 percent drop in circulation and 13 percent drop in revenues from 2017 to 2018 alone (Pew 2019). These dismal trends are also reflected in staffing: newsroom employment fell by 47 percent after 2004 (Pew 2019).

Between 2004 and 2018, 2,100 local newspapers closed, leaving 1,800 former newspaper communities without one (Abernathy 2020). The growing problem of newspaper closures and the news deserts they create is well-documented (e.g., Abernathy 2020; Ferrier et al. 2016):

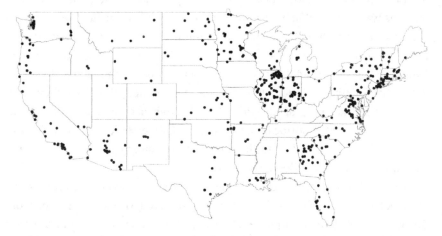

Figure 1 US local newspaper deaths, 2000–14. Data are drawn from the "Chronicling America" project, part of the National Digital Newspaper Program, which maintains a searchable database of the founding and folding dates of past and current US newspapers (Library of Congress 2016)

In the 15 years leading up to 2020, more than one-fourth of the country's newspapers disappeared, leaving residents in thousands of communities – inner-city neighborhoods, suburban towns and rural villages – living in vast news deserts. Simultaneously, half of all local journalists disappeared, as round after round of layoffs have left many surviving papers – the gutsy dailies and weeklies that had won accolades and Pulitzer Prizes for their reporting – mere "ghosts," or shells of their former selves. (Abernathy 2020)

Although local television remains the most popular news medium for most Americans, local television news also lost 14 percent of its audience in 2018. Local television newsrooms are producing more programming without spending more, forcing many stations into mergers and acquisitions: over 140 stations changed owners in 2018, at a cost of $8.8 billion dollars (Pew 2019).

Neither local newspapers nor television stations are financially succeeding in today's media marketplace, and many Americans are unaware of this crisis. According to Pew, 70 percent of Americans think their local news outlets are doing very well or somewhat well financially, and only 14 percent report that they paid for local news in the past year (Pew 2019). If the public remains unaware and unwilling to pay, we should expect local news to continue its steep decline.

2.3 Why National Cannot Replace Local

While local newspapers disappear, online news is proliferating. On television and in newspapers, local political news is accompanied by appealing and relevant information about local sports, shopping, businesses, and entertainment, as well as comics and crossword puzzles. Political content is less attractive once removed from that bundle (Hamilton 2004). As audiences abandon local newspapers for hyperlocal networks like NextDoor or Facebook groups (Molla 2019), they are unlikely to seek out local political information (Hamilton 2004). Instead, they will default to national news outlets, if, indeed, they seek any news replacements at all (Prior 2007). Audiences prefer stories about national news relative to local news when given the choice (Hopkins 2018), so, as local news availability declines, regular exposure to national news media should increase (Lelkes, Sood, and Iyengar 2017).

In this high-choice environment, Americans' motivations and preferences are more determinative of the information they receive (Arceneaux and Johnson 2013; Prior 2007; Delli Carpini et al. 1994). If they do not choose local news content, Americans may rely on partisanship and national news to inform their political decisions, even in elections those sources do not cover (Darr, Hitt, and Dunaway 2018; Hopkins 2018; Trussler 2018; Gerber, Kaplan, and Bergen 2009; Della Vigna and Kaplan 2007).

People whose primary news source is local know more about their local politicians than those who favor national news (Hopkins 2018; Shaker 2009; Mondak 1995). However, it is important to distinguish whether national news consumption actively detracts from local political knowledge, or merely adds nothing. Holding local news use constant, does more national news use lead to less overall knowledge of local politics?

Elections are crucial times for local media to cover politicians and their proposals because voters rely on the media to hear about their options (Levy and Squire 2000; Goldenberg and Traugott 1980). Keeping incumbents responsive requires strong challengers, who rely on local media coverage to inform voters about their candidacy and issue positions (Hayes and Lawless 2015; Cain, Ferejohn, and Fiorina 1987). The media environment influences candidate entry into elections, not just coverage of those candidates once declared (Arceneaux et al. 2020). Non-incumbents must rely more on local newspapers to spread their message (Hayes and Lawless 2018, 2015; Arnold 2004; Cook 1989), since they often lack the funds to advertise. Newspapers also cover non-incumbent candidates more extensively and positively than incumbents (Arnold 2004).

We therefore propose that national news cannot substitute for local news: *More local news exposure should make voters more familiar with local candidates, while additional national news exposure should not.*

2.3.1 Data, Methods, and Results

News media's impact on knowledge and opinions is difficult to determine without using an experiment, in which some people receive the media treatment and others do not. Experiments are easiest to conduct in a laboratory setting, although lab findings may not reflect the messier conditions of real-world news use. Local news users likely know more about local politics, but is that because they read the local news, or because they were interested enough to seek it out? In the following analyses, we use observational methods that provide us some insight into these questions even as they fundamentally cannot provide causal answers to our questions.

The first set of analyses, using cross-sectional surveys and fixed effects regressions, accounts for possible differences between congressional districts but cannot assess whether local news use is *causing* any statistically significant differences. The second, using panel data, is better because it measures changes over time within the same respondents. Even panel data are imperfect, however: the panel separates learning from pre-existing knowledge, but cannot separate learning from *interest in learning*. Unlike in Section 4, when we measure opinions before and after *The Desert Sun* changed its content, the following analyses can only tell us about how local and national news are associated with awareness of local politics and learning throughout an election.

Political awareness is measured using national items such as the balance of partisan power in Congress, partisan ideological distinctions (Delli Carpini and Keeter 1997), and knowledge of national current events and officials (Barabas et al. 2014; Barabas and Jerit 2009). Awareness of local politics is difficult to capture in a nationally representative survey because the correct answers vary greatly between areas (Shaker 2014). Recent research shows that local coverage of congressional elections increases awareness, but only examines willingness to offer opinions, not recall of candidates' names (Hayes and Lawless 2018, 2015).

We use data from the 2000 National Annenberg Election Survey (NAES), in which respondents were asked to name the candidates in their election for US Representative (a strict but common measure: see Snyder and Stromberg 2010; Hayes and Lawless 2018, 2015; Kam and Zechmeister 2013; Jacobson 2012; Arnold 2004; Vinson 2003; Mondak 1995;). Respondents' answers were recorded as verbatim text entries, including spelling mistakes and typos. We used a fuzzy substring matching algorithm to determine if the respondent named their candidate(s) correctly according to several standards of error and adopted the standard closest to a hand-coded subsample, resulting in a binary, replicable, original measure of local political knowledge in a national survey. Full details can be found in Appendix 2.B.[1] Name recall was low, at 14.5 percent of incumbents and 4.9 percent of nonincumbents.

National surveys generally ask about particular media, such as newspapers, television, radio, or the Internet, obscuring differences between local and national news sources and preferences. The 2000 NAES distinguished between national and local, allowing us to create an original index of local and national media use using self-reported days-per-week consumption of newspapers, television, and radio.[2]

Individual-level variables capturing politically relevant characteristics, potential influences on political learning, and partisanship were included in all logistic regression models (Zaller 1992). Variation between elections is

---

[1] All references to the Appendices refer to appendices that are hosted online.

[2] The national index includes reading a national newspaper, watching network television news, and watching cable television news, while the local index includes reading a local newspaper, watching local television news, and listening to talk radio, resulting in indices ranging from none (0) to daily consumption of all three types (1). Question wording for all variables used in these analyses can be found in Appendix 2C.

measured by variables for district competitiveness, if the election features an open seat, only one candidate, or a quality challenger, and a measure of district compactness (number of districts in a given media market; Campbell, Alford and Henry 1984). Candidate spending is also included to account for advertising (Jacobson 2012).[3]

We use logistic regression because our outcome variable is binary: either a respondent knows or does not know the candidate's name. The number of covariates in these analyses, detailed in above, means that our full tables would span several pages: we therefore include the full regression tables in the Appendix, along with a list of covariates and corresponding survey questions (Table 2.C1). The predicted probabilities with margins of error in Figure 2, used here because logistic regression coefficients are difficult to interpret substantively, give a sense of how our model predicts local political awareness changes as local and national news consumption increase and decrease, and how certain we are in those estimates based on our model.

Using more national news is associated with significantly lower recall of incumbent and non-incumbent House candidate names. Incumbent name recall drops 4.4 percent from no national news (15.1 percent) to maximum national news (10.7 percent), holding local news use at its mean. Non-incumbent candidate name recall drops from 5.3 percent to 2 percent along the same scale. Increased local news use, by the same token, is associated with an 8 percent increase in incumbent recall (no local news = 10.4 percent; maximum local news = 18.4 percent) and a 2.7 percent increase in non-incumbent recall (no local news = 3.2 percent; maximum local news = 5.9 percent). National and local news influence users in opposite directions: using more local news increases awareness of House candidates, while national news use is a detriment.

Next, we use panel data to isolate within-respondent changes in candidate name recall over the course of an election using repeated interviews. We use fixed-effects panel regression, which accounts for variables that do not change between panel waves (Allison 2009). These analyses therefore reflect within-respondent changes in House candidate name recall from before Labor Day, the traditional start of the fall campaign, to the month after election day, using the Multi-Reinterview Panel A from the 2000 NAES. The model accounts for relevant variables that may change between the panels: local and national

---

[3] Equation 1 estimates the relationship between the local and national media indices and local candidate name recall: $\Pr(\text{correct recall}) = f(\text{Local index} + \text{National index} + \Gamma_1 \text{Ind} + \Gamma_2 \text{CD} + \Gamma_3 \text{C and})$, where $\Pr(\text{correct recall})$ indicates the probability of correct recall of a candidate's name, Local index$_i$ represents the local news consumption index, National index represents the national news consumption index, CD is a set of congressional district-level control variables described above, C and is a set of congressional candidate-level control variables described above, and ε_i is a stochastic disturbance term.

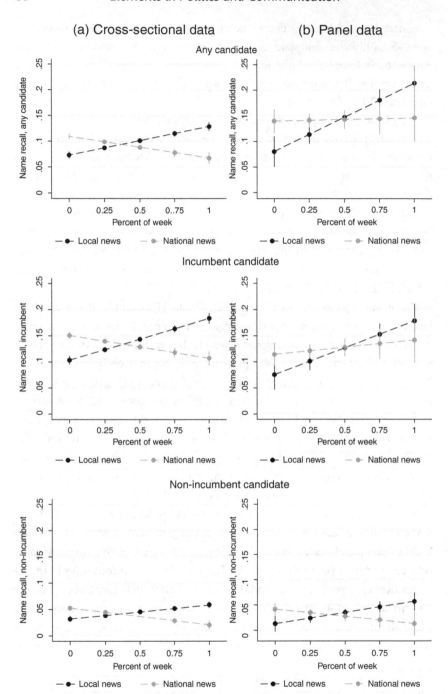

Figure 2 Predictions of local and national news consumption indices on House candidate name recall, (a) cross-sectional and (b) panel analyses using 2000 NAES

news consumption indices, online access, and political discussion with others. Column (b) of Figure 2 displays predicted probabilities describing the impact of levels of local and national news consumption in the panel analyses, with full results in Table 2.A3 of the Appendix.

Recall of any House candidate name increases along with local news use (no local news = 8 percent; maximum local news = 21.4 percent), while candidate recall stays flat as national news increases. Broken out into candidate types, moving from no local news to maximum local news exposure significantly increased recall by 10.3 percent for the incumbent (7.6 percent vs. 17.9 percent) and 4.4 percent for the non-incumbent(s) (1.3 percent vs. 5.7 percent; alpha = 0.05). More national news consumption increased incumbent recall slightly (2.7 percent, n.s.) while non-incumbent recall drops from 4.2 percent to 1.3 percent (n.s.). These decreases are not significant, tempering the conclusion from the first set of analyses (Figure 2a) that national news is actively detrimental. These findings clearly show, however, that national news does not help voters learn about local candidates.

These results are consistent with earlier work showing that when a local newspaper exits the marketplace, voters know less about local elections than voters in similar areas with newspapers (Mondak 1995). Although citizens may substitute to other forms of local media, such as local television news, they tend to lack the depth and breadth of local election coverage compared to newspapers (Mondak 1995). Local television news fails to provide comprehensive coverage of very competitive statewide elections, much less downballot races (Dunaway 2008; Kaplan et al. 2005). When races are uncompetitive or poorly funded, televised political ads are not available to inform voters. Similarly, when national news replaces local, subnational races go uncovered except in very special cases, hindering citizens' awareness and ability to hold downballot incumbents accountable (Arnold 2004; Mondak 1995).

Attention is a valuable resource, and choosing national news appears to actively distract from local politics (Stroud 2017). A healthy local media environment amplifies new candidates and local concerns. When today's interested consumers seek out the news, they often find national news instead, particularly online (Hindman 2011; Waldman 2011). As the balance of news options shifts towards national politics, these results warn us that national political news does not provide a desirable or acceptable substitute for local news.

2.4 Local News Is Less Polarizing

Unfortunately, declining political knowledge is not our only worry as audiences abandon local news: mounting evidence suggests that national news is more polarizing. Americans display the strongest relationship between trust and partisanship than any other people in the world: stronger partisans trust the news media less but trust their preferred outlets more (Suiter and Fletcher 2020). Polarization induced by national news may be self-reinforcing, causing a spiral of polarization. National outlets air more sound bites from politicians at the ideological extremes than from non-extremists (Padgett, Dunaway, and Darr 2019), and additional coverage of party conflict polarizes viewers (Levendusky and Malhotra 2015). In areas with worse coverage of local officials, such as those served by a media market in a different state, split-ticket voting is less common and voting is more nationalized (Moskowitz 2020).

In an appendix to our article about newspaper closures and polarization, we showed that national news contains more partisan cues than local news. Given the importance of this idea to our expectations about the *The Desert Sun*'s month-long vacation from national politics, we briefly summarize those analyses here. We used data from Gentzkow and Shapiro (2010; ICPSR file 26242–001-Data) containing newspaper-level measures of partisan slant based on a dictionary of partisan phrases used by members of Congress. Phrases used regularly by Democrats and not by Republicans were defined as Democratic phrases, and vice versa for Republicans. In 2005, Democrats more typically used phrases such as "workers' rights," "poor people," and "privatization plan," while Republicans more frequently said "stem cell," "personal retirement accounts," and "government spending" (Gentzkow and Shapiro 2010). These phrases reflect the battles over social security privatization and stem cell research that year, and clearly delineate where each side stood. The use of these phrases in news reporting allows us to assess the prevalence of partisan rhetoric.

The Gentzkow and Shapiro dataset includes counts of partisan phrases for more than 400 local daily newspapers, as well as the four leading national newspapers: the *New York Times*, the *USA Today*, the *Wall Street Journal*, and the *Washington Post*. Since national newspapers have larger circulations and space for news, we supplemented these data with newspaper circulation totals and a measure of each newspaper's total number of news articles published in 2005.[4] We used a negative binomial count regression modeling total number of partisan cues in the Gentzkow and Shapiro data, from 2000 to 2005, as a function of being a national newspaper and the logarithm of circulation size in 2005.[5]

---

[4] We base this measure of the "news hole" of each newspaper on Hayes and Lawless' (2018) method, which finds the total number of news articles published by newspapers in a given year by limiting article searches in the news archive database to year and paper only. Although this measure produces some error due to slight differences in how papers archive articles (see Hayes and Lawless 2018), it is the most reliable way we know to account for the size of a newspaper's space for news articles. See also Darr (2018).

[5] We used the "offset" function of the nbreg command in Stata to account for the available space for news in each newspaper (measured by the natural logarithm of the total number of articles on

In Table 1, we show a positive and significant effect for national newspapers, even while controlling for circulation rates, indicating that national newspapers contained substantially more partisan content than local newspapers. Predicted marginal effects, presented in Figure 3, show just how much: the national newspapers published, on average, over 40,000 partisan phrases from 2000–5, compared to an average of just over 15,000 in the same period for an average local newspaper.

Using an objective measure of partisan content from Gentzkow and Shapiro (2010), these analyses show that national newspapers use many more partisan phrases than do local newspapers, providing an empirical basis for our expectation that national political news is more polarizing than local news. The divisive and partisan nature of national news is becoming clearer as its position in the marketplace of news is becoming more dominant. The continued health and existence of local news is a useful bulwark against the divisiveness and gridlock that define American politics today.

2.5 Local Matters

Local newspapers matter and provide information that is better than national news at informing citizens about the government and their representatives and

Table 1 Partisan phrases in national newspapers compared to partisan phrases in local newspapers, 2000–5. Negative binomial regression, offset using the natural logarithm of the 2005 total published articles to constrain coefficient to 1. Standard errors in parentheses.

	(1)
	Total key partisan phrases, 2000–5
National newspaper	0.948***
	(0.258)
Log(Circulation)	0.026
	(0.024)
Constant	−0.709***
	(0.263)
Observations	317

*** $p < 0.01$, ** $p < 0.05$, * $p < 0.1$. Originally published in the online appendix to "Newspaper Closures Polarize Voting Behavior," by Darr, Hitt, and Dunaway, *Journal of Communication*, 2018. Available at https://doi.org/10.1093/joc/jqy051

Newsbank for each newspaper in 2005), and control for circulation to account for the resources available to each newspaper.

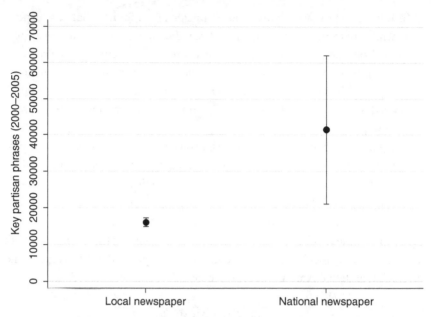

Figure 3 Predicted marginal effects of partisan phrases in national and local newspapers, 2000–5. Data from Gentzkow and Shapiro (2010), ICPSR data file 26242–001-Data. Figure originally published in the appendix to "Newspaper Closures Polarize Voting Behavior," by Darr, Hitt, and Dunaway, *Journal of Communication*, 2018

does so in a less polarizing way that does not focus on party conflict. Local reporters and editors have the expertise and incentives to keep their community informed. The research discussed in this Section shows that political knowledge, engagement, and accountability will suffer if local news declines further.

The Desert Sun focused on the distinction between national and local when it announced its plans to drop national content from the opinion page in July, allowing for a rare direct test of the polarizing influence of national content. Op-ed page material is different from hard news found in other sections of the paper, and the evidence we present here is about hard news. Why should we expect to observe effects from the absence of national op-ed material?

There are several reasons to anticipate effects from changes to the op-ed page. First, while op-ed content and hard news are not the same, they share many similarities. Despite the storied "impenetrable wall" that is supposed to exist between the hard news departments and the editorial departments in a newspaper, the wall is somewhat porous, at least regarding newspapers' coverage of endorsed candidates (Kahn and Kenney 2002). Second, although hard news might be more trusted and persuasive because it is ostensibly neutral, and thereby consumed less defensively than opinion content, fact-based reporting often lacks the argumentation or substance necessary for capturing the levels of attention required for persuasion (Dunaway et al. 2015). Third, elite cues substantially impact the strength of mass partisanship (Hetherington 2001), sorting (Levendusky 2009; Layman and Carsey 2002), and polarization (Baldassarri and Gelman 2008). The observed polarized and sorted patterns in the electorate may simply reflect an improved ability to use elite partisan dues to distinguish between increasingly polarized parties (Darr and Dunaway 2018; Prior 2013). Given that the op-ed page is full of elite cues, we should expect the presence or absence of national politics there to affect polarization.

In other words, local opinion matters, too. Next, we will show that removing national politics reordered the priorities of the opinion page, and the attitudes of Palm Springs residents, by bringing opinion back home and deemphasizing party politics.

3 How the Opinion Page Changed

> As force is always on the side of the governed, the governors have nothing to support them but opinion. It is, therefore, on opinion that government is founded; and this maxim extends to the most despotic and the most military governments as well as to the most free and most popular. – David Hume (cited in Innis 1951)

When *The Desert Sun* announced its intention to take a "summer vacation" from national politics, Executive Editor Julie Makinen thought that readers might find it jarring: "What will I do for a month without Marc Thiessen, or Leonard Pitts? What will we talk about, if not Donald Trump and Nancy Pelosi?" (Makinen 2019a). National politics is central to political considerations across all levels of government in America today (Hopkins 2018), and it is hard to discuss politics at any level without mentioning the president, Congress, or partisan conflict.

Did *The Desert Sun* follow through on its commitment to home style opinion, or was it too difficult? What filled the substantial hole in opinion page content left by the removal of nationally framed op-eds, editorials, and letters? How much national content was replaced by state and local topics? Which issues and perspectives received more or less attention?

In this Section, we show that national politics was successfully dropped in July, which represented a substantial change from other months. Nearly all op-eds, editorials, and letters published in July ignored national politics and focused on local subjects. Nationally syndicated columnists regularly appeared on *The Desert Sun*'s opinion page in June and August, but not in July. Mentions of President Trump, who normally dominates the news (Confessore and Younish 2016), essentially disappeared. Syndicated coverage decreased overall as the newspaper relied more heavily on columns about California from the statewide service CALmatters. Locals voiced their concerns loudly throughout July: architectural restoration, downtown redevelopment, traffic, development, environmental issues, and education received more attention, while the nationalized issue of immigration largely disappeared from the opinion page.

July also exposed the widespread deficit of diversity on opinion pages. Editors want to ensure perspectives from across the left-right ideological axis, but historically, there are serious disparities in the representation of racial minorities and women on opinion pages. American newspapers typically amplify elite voices and entrenched political interests (Hindman 2018; Davis 1999; Abramson et al. 1988; Innis 1951), a fact reflected in an overrepresentation of white male authors (Page 1996). We wanted to examine whether localization had "spillover" effects of making the opinion page more representative of the region. We find no evidence that localization improved gender equality or racial diversity: women continued to be underrepresented, as did Hispanic/Latino writers, who did not contribute to opinion in proportion to their population in the area.

The opinion page also included more messages from executives, politicians, and corporations in July. For example, the syndication service CALmatters supplied many more columns about California state politics, but usually from the perspective of lobbyists, interest groups, or politicians. While the topics discussed in July were undeniably more local, more elites were also represented.

The July opinion page experiment was a dramatic change for readers, and the newspaper followed through on its daunting commitment. The lessons from July showcase some of the promises and pitfalls facing other newspapers looking to localize.

3.1 The Opinion Page

We focus on the effects of a one-month change in the opinion page of *The Desert Sun*: no other parts of the newspaper were affected in the month of July. The opinion page includes editorials, op-eds, and letters to the editor. In editorials, a newspaper speaks with authority about issues of its choosing, while op-ed pieces are frequently written by non-staff contributors. Nearly every major newspaper publishes two to three op-eds per day, some publish daily editorials, and others (like *The Desert Sun*) publish editorials only occasionally (Sommer and Maycroft 2008). Opinion pages can influence readers, hold newspaper staffers accountable, and make community journalism work better, but realizing that potential takes effort from editors. The history of the op-ed page shows why the opinion section matters, in spite of only comprising one page on most days in *The Desert Sun*.

Op-ed ("opposite the editorial") pages began in 1970, when the *New York Times* carved out space for outside writers with views that would "very frequently be divergent from [their] own" (Shipley 2004). The *Times* envisioned that "the two pages together – Editorial and Op. Ed. – are designed to create an intellectual forum from which . . . nothing will be foreign that relates to man and his society" (New York Times 1970). Diversity of viewpoints proved valuable for newspapers seeking out new readers and advertisers (Rosenfeld 2000), even if the writers were overwhelmingly white and male (Wolf 1995).

The op-ed page involves readers in community discourse (Ciofalo and Traverso 1994), helps the general public interpret current events, sets the news and policy agenda, and ensures that non-journalist perspectives appear in the newspaper (Socolow 2010; Sommer and Maycroft 2008). Media help the public navigate the political world, and op-ed perspectives (Wood and Porter 2019; Nyhan and Reifler 2010) and endorsements (Ladd and Lenz 2009) are particularly powerful guides. Those who read persuasive op-eds durably change their opinions in the intended direction: "In the setting of newspaper op-eds, individuals are capable of considering diverse views and may perhaps even change their minds" (Coppock et al. 2018).

In national politics, op-ed pages have been criticized for overrepresenting the views of political elites and failing to represent a full array of perspectives on major political issues. Operating within a two major party system, news outlets' tendency to rely on political elite viewpoints reduces most op-ed page debates down to only two perspectives, a process known as "indexing" (Page 1996). This bias toward elite perspectives can be attributed in part to the fact that opinion editors balance the need for regular publication against maintaining editorial standards. The values that make an op-ed submission attractive to editors resemble the attributes of a good news story: a column should be "newsy, consequential, argued rather than asserted, stylish . . . reasonably convincing in its conclusion," and, most importantly, "delivered in a timely fashion by e-mail, normally seven hundred words, clean, and double-spaced" (Rosenfeld 2000). Submissions with these attributes require less effort from editors, increasing the odds of publication. Elites, if they are not writers or former journalists themselves, often have the benefit of working with public relations professionals who know how to satisfy most of those criteria while advocating for their cause or industry, making opinion editors vulnerable to their influence. Think tanks, industry associations, business groups, politicians, public relations agencies, and academics submit to op-ed pages regularly, knowing editors may prefer a professionally edited piece from a CEO over a rougher first-time attempt from a local resident.

Makinen clearly wanted submissions from the community, explicitly asking readers: "To make this monthlong vacation a reality, we need your help. This is an open call for YOU to submit pieces to us for publication" (Makinen 2019a). The newspaper repeated these calls on June 30 and July 1, on the opinion page and with personal appeals from Makinen herself:

> I personally sent a lot of emails to people telling them that we were doing this and we wanted it to be a success . . . if I had met them for lunch or I had met them at a community meeting, just asking them, hey, we talked about X, Y, and Z. Could you write 500 words about that? . . . And I was pleasantly surprised. (Makinen, personal communication, June 18, 2020)

The Desert Sun's opinion page generally consists of two or three editorial-length submissions (around 500–550 words, according to their guidelines), a cartoon, and two to five letters to the editor. Some days had no letter to the editor, while Sundays featured between eight and ten. "Valley Voice"/"Your Turn" columns "address a political or social issue at the state or local level," and writers were encouraged to "stick to a single topic and avoid personal attacks." Letters to the editor were restricted to verifiable residents of the newspaper's circulation area, although there were a few exceptions. The newspaper did not accept more than one letter or column from any contributor in July.

The opinion page is edited and regulated according to clear rules, and enforcing those rules requires effort from dedicated editors. Regulations encouraged local participation and topics and discouraged promotional content and uncivil discourse. The July experiment merely extended these rules to ban national politics.

3.2 What Changed in July?

Articles were coded according to contributors' locality, diversity, and authority, and stories were classified by topics. Trained research assistants and an author classified the full set of articles from the opinion page in PDFs of the print editions of *The Desert Sun* in June, July, and August of 2019. The author's coding is used for the analyses except where noted. Pieces were coded for attributes of their authors and content, particularly the locality of stories and authors, race and gender of authors, and the issues discussed.[6]

---

[6] We did not distinguish between regional, state, and "local" stories because the editors' distinction was between national and subnational. We did not code for the ideological lean of the op-eds (Wagner and Collins 2014), although this could be an interesting direction for future research.

Research assistants determined whether an author lived in California and entered a title and affiliated organization if given. Op-ed authors were frequently accompanied by pictures, and coders assessed authors' race and gender based on a combination of the author's name, picture, and research as necessary. For letters to the editor, it was not possible to determine race, but gender was coded according to coders' impressions of an author's first name. When clear, gender was coded: ambiguous names, and entries written by an editorial board (*The Desert Sun* or syndicated editorials) were left blank.[7]

Issue topics were determined by coding randomly selected out-of-sample months inductively: research assistants created ten to twelve categories that were most commonly discussed in their month (September 2018 and March 2019). These categories were then used to categorize stories in the summer months of 2019 and 2018. These issue categories included the following topics: immigration, elections, education, Trump, whether the story mentioned any politician, budget/economy, environment, art and culture, health, transportation, and crime/guns. A story could be classified as discussing more than one issue.[8]

The research design for our survey analyses, described in the next chapter, depends on July being distinctive for the readers of *The Desert Sun* opinion page. In the language of social scientific jargon, we need a manipulation check to ensure that national politics was actually removed. We examine three areas to verify this—syndication, local stories, and stories about President Trump—and assess differences using t-tests comparing July stories to the pooled stories of June and August.

3.2.1 Syndication: Less National, More State

We first examine changes in syndicated columns. If the newspaper barely used nationally syndicated writers previously, or already relied extensively on locally syndicated content, the July experiment may not have changed the opinion page much. Nationally syndicated content in June and August included columns from other editorial boards, conservative columnists such as Cal Thomas and Marc Thiessen, and liberals including E.J. Dionne and Esther Cepeda.

---

[7] There were twenty-eight "editorial board"-authored pieces out of 238 total op-eds, or 11 percent of the sample, with no ambiguous gender codes. Among letters, only nineteen out of 216 (8.8 percent) of authors had gender-ambiguous first names.

[8] Intercoder agreement was calculated using Cohen's kappa, and was generally acceptable for the variables presented: syndication (0.959), California topics (0.844), Trump mentions (0.811), art and culture (0.603), transportation (0.794), education (0.575), environment (0.693), immigration (0.718), woman author (0.905), white author (0.824), Black author (0.884), and Hispanic author (0.803). Full details on intercoder agreement can be found in the Appendix in Table A.31.

Syndication delivered California content through the nonprofit, grant-supported service CALmatters, which supplies state politics columns to local newspapers across the state. The most consistent CALmatters contributor was Dan Walters, a longtime journalist for the *Sacramento Bee* who has written about California politics since 1981 (CALmatters 2020). His column appears, on average, once every three days in *The Desert Sun*, making him the most frequent contributor to the opinion page over the three months examined.

In June and August 2019, the op-eds on the opinion page were syndicated more than two-thirds of the time: 68 percent in June and 69 percent in August (combined M = 0.685, SD = 0.46). In July, that proportion dropped to 38 percent (SD = 0.49), a significant dip (t(236) = 4.53, p < 0.000). The newspaper filled a syndication gap of approximately 30 percent with local coverage in July, as shown in Figure 4.

The Desert Sun more than doubled the number of CALmatters columns to fill this gap. State-level syndicated columns went from 16 percent in June to 37.5 (SD = 0.49) percent in July and back down to 20.5 percent in August (M combined June and August = 0.183, SD = 0.39), a significant difference (t(234) = –3.23, p < 0.001). This was not due to more Walters columns (nine in June, eight in July, nine in August): instead, sixteen of the twenty-four CALmatters op-eds in July were by guest contributors, compared to only two

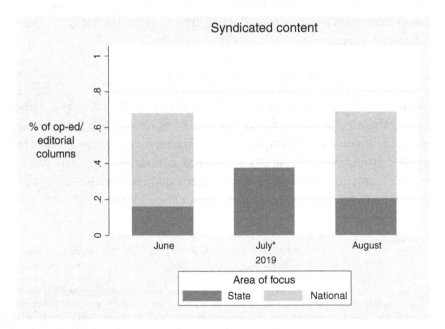

Figure 4 Syndicated content with a national or state focus, by month

of eleven in June and only five of fourteen in August. July's reliance on CALmatters is problematic for reasons we will explore later, but the service clearly helped the newspaper achieve their goals.

3.2.2 More California, Less Trump

Local topics dominated the opinion page in July, as promised. Typically, *The Desert Sun*'s op-eds, editorials, and letters concerned subnational topics less than half the time. In July, 96 percent (SD = 0.19) of the opinion page dealt with California and Coachella Valley topics, double the coverage of the months surrounding it (t(236) = –8.78, p < 0.000). Figure 5 shows that editorials and letters followed this same pattern, with few differences across those two categories of content.

Only 36 percent of op-eds and editorials in June were locally focused, while half were local in August (M combined = 0.43, SD = 0.5). Letters were

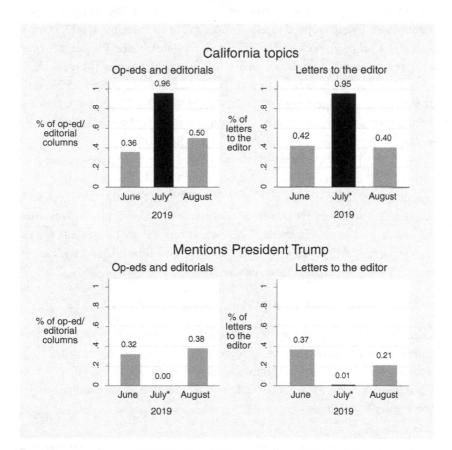

Figure 5 California and Trump content, by month

particularly localized: only 42 percent in June and 40 percent in August were locally focused (M combined = 41.4, SD = 0.49), but that jumped to 95 percent in July (SD = 0.21; t(214) = −9.67, p < 0.000). It is easy to assume that local newspapers publish opinions on mostly local issues. In June and August, around six in ten letters were about nonlocal topics. Many readers express their opinions on national issues in their local newspaper.

Opinion page content mentioning President Trump, a polarizing politician with unprecedented earned media exposure (Confessore and Younish 2016), is a useful metric for coverage of national politics. All modern presidents try to earn national media coverage to gain leverage on Congress, states, and federal agencies (Kernell 2006; Neustadt 1980). Presidents may also "go local" to earn support in specific localities, through travel or targeted messaging (Cohen 2010; Eshbaugh-Soha 2010). Focusing on reported news misses the president's substantial presence on the opinion page.

Approximately one-third of all opinion page content mentioned President Trump in June and August (M combined = 35.2, SD = 0.48), but opinion page mentions of Trump dropped to zero in July (t(236) = 6.26, p < 0.000). True to Makinen's promise, none of the op-eds in July mentioned President Trump, a big change from 32 percent in June and 38 percent in August (M combined = 35.1, SD = 0.48). There was more variety in letters to the editor, although the decrease was still significant (t(214) = 5.85, p < 0.000): 37 percent mentioned Trump in June, compared to only 21 percent in August (M combined = 30.5, SD = 0.46) with nearly nothing in July (M = 0.01, SD = 0.11).

July's experiment disrupted the usual balance of local and national content. The hole left by dropping national syndication was filled with locally focused op-eds and letters, leading to the banishment of Trump from the opinion page. In the summer of an odd-numbered year, there were no local elections in June, July, or August in the Coachella Valley, while national political events such as the Democratic primary raged on. As such, electoral politics took a back seat to intensely local issues and citizen concerns.[9]

3.3 Amplifying Local Issues

Palm Springs is known for its thriving art, theatre, and music scenes, and is an architectural destination for its "mid-century modern" houses and buildings. Several organizations in Palm Springs, such as the Palm Springs Preservation Foundation and the Palm Springs Modern Committee, are committed to preserving these buildings.

---

[9] If a newspaper were willing, it would be informative to replicate this experiment during the month before a national election.

The conversation about arts and culture centered on a building called the Town & Country Center (T&CC) in downtown Palm Springs, an issue that touches on race, local politics, crime, and many other aspects of local politics. The T&CC was designed in 1948 by Paul R. Williams, the first Black member of the American Institute of Architects, and A. Quincy Jones (Robinson-Jacobs 2020). Gary Johns, president of the Palm Springs Preservation Foundation, referred to the T&CC as "a true architectural gem" in a June 30 op-ed (Johns 2019): "[O]ne of the best examples of the international-style of architecture in southern California" and "architecturally noteworthy for its pedestrian-friendly courtyard" (Palm Springs Preservation Foundation 2020).

In 2019, the T&CC was caught up in a negotiation around a previous violation of California Code 1090, a statute preventing officials from contracting with companies in which they have a financial interest. Former Mayor Steve Pougnet was indicted along with two developers under public corruption charges including dealings on the $400 million downtown redevelopment project. Section 1090 violations render void any contracts linked to wrongdoing by officials, so lawyers for the development company negotiated by offering valuable land to the city. The July 7 editorial specifically mentions the letters asking for the T&CC to be included, and the editorial board agreed (The Desert Sun 2019).

Letters about the T&CC dominated early July, with twenty-five published in the first half of the month. On Saturday, July 6, all four letters advocated including the building in the 1090 settlement. The next day, a Sunday, all ten letters said the same. More appeared on July 9 (two), July 10 (two), July 12 (three), and Sunday, July 14 (four). There was no balance or rebuttal: the letters exclusively wanted the T&CC included in the 1090 settlement. Overall, arts and culture significantly increased ($t(214) = -6.03$, $p < 0.000$) to 28 percent of all letters in July (SD = 0.45), compared to 4 percent in June and none in August (M combined = 0.023, SD = 0.15).

The Palm Springs Preservation Foundation inspired enough letters to dominate the letters section and influence *The Desert Sun*'s editorial board. The developers' proposals included other land set to be used for conservation – a frequent topic of the opinion page – but environmental groups did not coalesce behind that perspective publicly. The extra opinion space in July amplified architectural preservation instead.

Letters to the editor about transportation issues jumped to 25 percent of all letters in July (SD = 0.44), a significant increase ($t(214) = -3.58$, $p < 0.000$) from 11 percent in June and 4 percent in August (M combined = 0.08, SD = 0.27). Op-eds and editorials on this topic stayed steady, with 7 percent of op-eds and editorials were about transportation in July compared to 5 percent in June and 2 percent in August. Californians care about transportation and traffic: congested roads, road safety, and drunk driving were major letter topics in July (see Figure 6).

The two major topics of discussion in letters to the editor were the construction of a new arena near the Agua Caliente casino in downtown Palm Springs, and the "CVLink," an in-progress pedestrian, bicycle, and "low-speed electric vehicle" pathway between the cities in the Coachella Valley Association of Governments, a regional planning agency coordinating government services in the area (CVAG 2016, 2015).

The cities of Indian Wells and Rancho Mirage opposed the CVLink, as detailed in an editorial by *The Desert Sun.* Indian Wells voters prohibited development of the CVLink in their town, but La Quinta wanted the trail and needed to annex a small portion of Indian Wells as part of the development. *The*

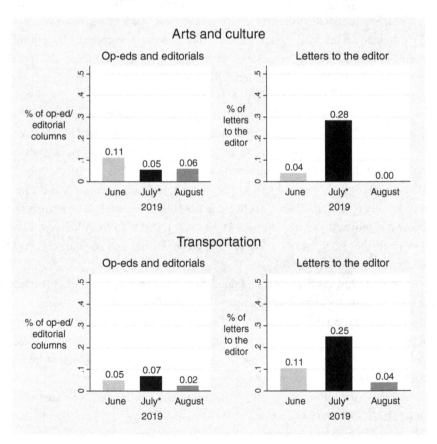

Figure 6 Arts and culture and transportation content, by month

Desert Sun editorial board approved of the CVLink and hoped the two towns could come to an agreement (June 13, The Desert Sun 2019). Unlike with the T&CC, there were multiple perspectives about CVLink. Many were opposed, arguing that the "$100 million sidewalk folly" (June 23, McQuary 2019) cut through areas where people experiencing homelessness live, failed to produce the promised renewable solar energy, and created traffic and parking hassles (June 27, Clapp 2019; July 31, Miringoff 2019). Those in favor of the CVLink, including a member of the "Friends of CV Link" board, argued that it would make bicyclists safer and accused the opposed cities of stoking "false fears in the name of elitism and unfounded expenses of operation" (July 21, Lueders 2019; July 25, Yepello 2019).

The new arena was planned by the local Agua Caliente Band of Cahuilla Indians on land next to their casino. It was a joint venture of the National Hockey League (NHL), which awarded a minor league American Hockey League (AHL) affiliate of the new Seattle expansion franchise to Palm Springs on June 26, 2019, and Live Nation, which agreed to supply the arena with touring musical acts and events (Baker 2019). The NHL deal was announced in late June, which likely also influenced the surge of letters. Most letters about the new arena opposed it on the basis of traffic. Many brought up broader tensions with the tribe, including complaints that "the city . . . allows the sovereign nation carte blanche exemption from local controls" (July 9, Marksbury 2019), and "the tribe wants to change our peaceful way of life by bringing Los Angeles traffic to Palm Springs" (July 9, Talmy 2019).

Traffic is a common theme in letters to the editor throughout the summer, as shown by headlines like "Traffic safety is vital in the desert" (July 1, Whetstone 2019); "Rules keep our roads safe" (July 16, MacFarlane 2019); and "Enough, road warriors" (July 25, Grine 2019). Traffic was linked to tourism, the engine of the local economy: "[O]ne experience with the gridlock that will definitely ensue will be enough to discourage future attendees and general downtown visitors" (July 15, Austin and Bronat 2019). Any news about events that might increase traffic will lead to letters, and those submissions found more space in July.

Transportation is central to politics and everyday life in Palm Springs and the Coachella Valley. CVLink and the new arena fueled citizen concerns that were expressed in the opinion page, with some encouragement from elites. The back-and-forth on CVLink seemed to be influenced by elected officials, editorials, and pro-CVLink organizations, while opposition to the arena came from traffic concerns. Cues from the newspaper's editorial board and elected officials, combined with space to discuss a "chronically accessible" issue like traffic, led to more conversation in July.

3.3.1 Education, the Environment, and Immigration

Education and the environment were featured in twice the number of op-eds in July (M = 13.7, SD = 0.35) as in June or August (M combined = 0.07, SD = 0.25), a weakly significant increase (t(236) = −1.77, p = 0.07), but experienced no significant change in letters. July had more original local input on education from area elites in op-eds but still mostly featured syndicated content, a contrast with op-eds discussing the environment, of which half of the op-eds in July were non-syndicated.

Immigration has both national and local angles for *The Desert Sun*. California has more immigrants than any other state: 27 percent of the state is foreign-born, more than half the state's immigrants are naturalized US citizens, and another 25 percent have another legal status such as green cards or visas (Johnson and Sanchez 2019). President Trump routinely discusses immigration using polarizing and inflammatory language (Sides, Vavreck, and Tesler 2018). Would July's experiment lead to an influx of local immigration stories and issues, or is the issue so nationalized that it cannot easily be discussed without referencing Trump? (See Figure 7.)

Across all three months, there were very few original, local op-eds about education. School is not in session during summer months, but school policy is newsworthy year-round. There were ten op-eds about education in July, compared to five in June and six in August. All education op-eds in June and August were syndicated, and seven of ten in July were from CALmatters. The three original local op-eds were by educators: an adjunct professor at College of the Desert in Palm Desert talking about music education (July 15, Bakal 2019); the superintendent of the Palm Springs Unified School District discussing truancy (July 19, Lyon 2019), and a Palm Springs Unified School District Foundation (a 501(c)3 organization supporting the schools) board member writing about including the Agua Caliente tribe in the local curriculum (July 30, Blumberg 2019).

Original local op-eds about the environment dealt with the environmental threats that accompany living in the desert, including earthquakes and water resources. The editorial board set the tone with a July 1 editorial about Nestlé's harvesting of local spring water under a "decades-old, long expired permit, at the cost of a few hundred dollars per year" (The Desert Sun 2019). The mayor pro tem of Rancho Mirage wrote about using salt water from the Sea of Cortez, rather than freshwater from the imperiled Salton Sea, as a water resource (July 28, Hobart 2019). Other op-eds discussed bighorn sheep, from a member of the board of directors of Palm Desert's Bighorn Institute (July 19, Rickin 2019), and the restorative effects of hiking (July 24, Seeger 2019).

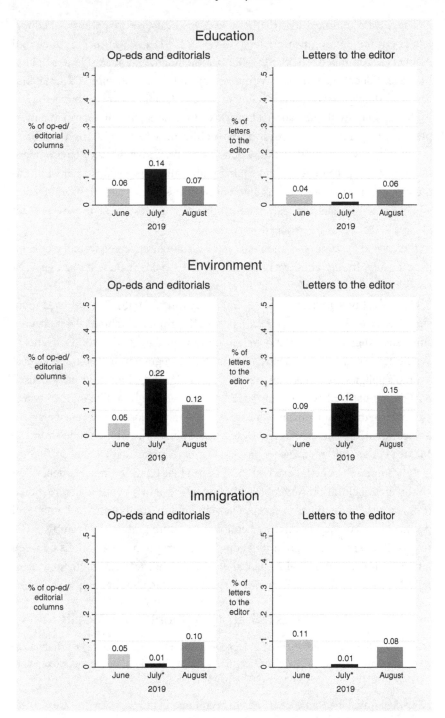

Figure 7 Education, environment, and immigration content, by month

There were significantly (t(236) = –2.92, p = 0.004) more op-eds and editorials about the environment in July (M = 0.22, SD = 0.42) than in June and August (M combined = 0.08, SD = 0.28), although the number of letters did not increase. Education and the environment are relevant statewide. CALmatters' focus on state government inevitably includes education, a major budget priority for the state with the nation's largest (California State University) and most prestigious (University of California) public university systems (Cal State 2020; UC Newsroom 2019). Many policies are framed in terms of environmental impact and green energy, in keeping with California's status as an environmental leader on topics such as automobile emissions (Irfan 2019). Education and the environment are perpetually important issues, even if they are not always at the top of the readers' mind.

Letters and op-eds about immigration practically disappeared from the opinion page in July. Immigration was the topic of few op-eds in June and August (M combined = 0.07, SD = 0.26). In July, that fell to one percent (M = 0.01, SD = 0.12), a weakly significant drop (t(236) = 1.85, p = 0.065). The fall was more significant with letters (t(214) = 2.53, p = 0.012), from a combined 9.4 percent in June and August (SD = 0.29) to 1.1 percent in July (SD = 0.11). National syndicated columnists frequently wrote about immigration, both for and against Trump's policies, and those columns disappeared in July. Letters in June focused on Trump's national policies, and so did not appear in July. While immigration is currently an important human rights issue, it may not be locally relevant enough to attract significant attention in *The Desert Sun*: Palm Springs is 125 miles from the Mexico border, not immediately proximate to it (Branton and Dunaway 2009).

July's opinion page focused on local issues that Palm Springs residents care about: architectural preservation, building an arena, negotiating a recreational trail, and protecting bighorn sheep. These issues are deeply entwined with local politics, even if they are not as "political" as immigration or Trump's latest tweets. Readers could learn a lot about local corruption, negotiations between city governments, the local Agua Caliente tribe, and state environmental regulations by seeing these topics more frequently on the Opinion page.

3.4 Who Benefits? Diversity, Authority, and Locality

Not only is information a tool and resource used by political actors in a strategic or psychological sense, its characteristics and qualities help define political actors themselves. – Bruce Bimber (2003, p. 231)

Historical imbalances in access and voice endured in the pages of *The Desert Sun* during 2019 and this was unchanged in July: 22 percent of op-ed columns in June were written by women, compared to 21 percent in July and 18 percent in August.

Letters to the editor were more representative in June: 40 percent of the letters to the editor in June were by women, which fell to 32 percent in July and 23 percent in August. June's proportion of letters to the editor matches the composition of the city of Palm Springs (only 41 percent female; U.S. Census Bureau 2019), but the gender ratio slipped out of proportion in July and August. Gender equality was not an explicit goal or an unintended benefit of the experiment, but it did not improve (see Figure 8).

Palm Springs is a largely white community: 83.3 percent according to the Census, with 27.8 percent of the population identifying as Hispanic or Latino. Nearby cities such as Cathedral City (59.6 percent) and Indio (65.6 percent), have much larger Hispanic or Latinx populations, while Palm Desert (25.5 percent) resembles Palm Springs. None is more than 4 percent Black: even very low levels of Black authorship are "proportional" in the Coachella Valley. Given that white and Hispanic/Latinx were not separate variables in the coding scheme, white writers were determined by coders to be "white alone," a category that the U.S. Census says describes only 60.7 percent of Palm Springs. In Cathedral City (30.4 percent "white alone") and Indio (28.3 percent), the disparity is starker.

White authors wrote 81 percent of op-eds in June and 82 percent in August. In July, however, this number jumped to 92 percent. Nationally syndicated columnists such as Esther Cepeda, Leonard Pitts, and others represented some of the only Black and Hispanic op-ed contributors in *The Desert Sun*. These authors often wrote about their racial and ethnic communities, but

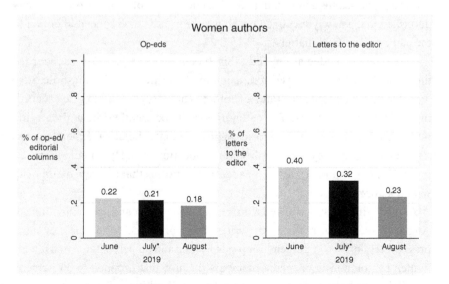

Figure 8 Content authored by women, by month

always at a national scale and often in the context of Trump's policies. Local perspectives from racial and ethnic minority authors were lacking and did not increase in July (see Figure 9).

Op-eds with nonlocal topics had roughly 2.5 times the number of Hispanic authors over the entire summer as did local topics (15.6 percent vs. 6.7 percent). Nationally syndicated columnist Esther Cepeda alone made up nearly one-third of the op-eds by Hispanics over the summer. The presence of Spanish-language and bilingual newspapers in the Coachella Valley means that *The Desert Sun* could do more Hispanic outreach, but the drop in July reveals that local Hispanic perspectives are not part of their opinion page strategy.

Overall, racial and ethnic disparities endured for the area's largest ethnic minority, while women authors remained disadvantaged as opinion page contributors. Local writers in July remained mostly male, with more columns by white authors and somewhat fewer by Hispanic and Latino authors.

3.4.1 Authority: More Executives, Fewer Journalists in July

When editors seek more freelance and locally written pieces, they risk influence by public relations professionals enlisted to help business executives reach readers (Ciofalo and Traverso 1994; Joyce 1990). Opening up the opinion page may result in replacement writers who are "the connected [and] the credentialed" and have "establishment expertise" and "celebrity or prominence" (Seldner 1994). The opinion page both confers status on its authors and rewards higher-status authors. In this subsection, we explore the titles of authors published in the newly localized opinion page in July, with special attention to the authors from CALmatters.

Titles were provided at the end of each column in italics. Coders recorded the author's title as it was written, using the first title named if multiple titles were listed. Five categories (and an "other" category) classified titles according to professional status. The categories included whether the author's title portrayed them in several categories: a government official; an expert, such as a professor; simply by their profession or location (other); a media member, journalist, or columnist; or as an executive, for titles that conveyed authority within an organization.

Authors' titles in July showed a different mix of power and status than June or August. Usually, the majority of writers are journalists, columnists, or other press professionals: 75 percent of op-eds in June and 68 percent in August were written by columnists or media members. In July, that dropped to 33 percent. Localizing the opinion page also de-professionalized it (see Figure 10).

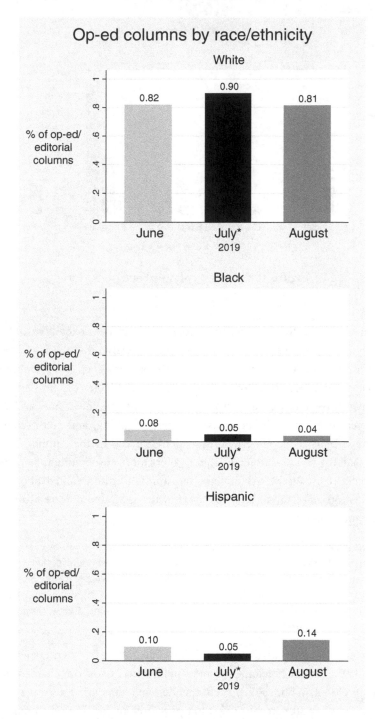

Figure 9 Content authored by white, Black, and Hispanic authors, by month

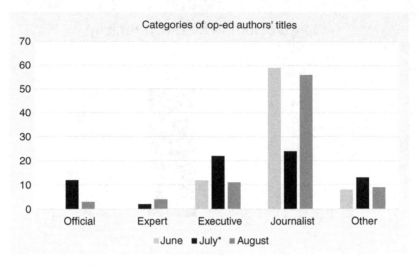

Figure 10 Categories of op-ed authors' titles

That space was filled by public officials and business executives. Op-eds by public officials went from none in June to twelve in July, and dropped down to three in August, from an array of positions such as assemblyman, city councilor, library director, and mayor pro tem. Elected officials promoted their own bills, publicized their accomplishments and positions, and doing what elected officials do: advertising, position-taking, and credit-claiming (Mayhew 1974). Encountering these perspectives in the opinion section rather than the news section may make voters more susceptible to persuasion (Coppock et al. 2018). Al Franco, the opinion editor, talked about self-interested op-eds from officials as "part of the job," and deferred to readers to interpret columns:

> Ideally, if they're making an argument and it's clearly identified – by the way, this was from the president of the state employee, whatever union or this is the president of the Natural Gas Producers Association or whatever – as long as that's there and it's clear, I have to believe that our readers know that, and that this is a message from someone who obviously has a point of view. (Franco, personal conversation, June 18, 2020)

There were more executives on the opinion page in July, from writers with titles including California director, CEO and chief innovation officer, chair and CEO, head of global public policy, and founder and director. Executive-written columns rose to 30 percent of opinion page columns in July, doubling other months' totals of 15 percent (June) and 13 percent (August). While business and advocacy groups' perspectives are consequential, the fact that more executives were published spotlights a tradeoff in the opinion page: efforts to include more statewide and community voices can increase the power of elites.

3.4.2 Case Study: CALmatters and the Problem of Public Relations

CALmatters, the statewide syndication service, helped powerful Californian voices reach *The Desert Sun*'s readers in July. In its own words, "CALmatters is a nonpartisan, nonprofit journalism venture committed to explaining how California's state Capitol works and why it matters" (Institute for Nonprofit News 2020). CALmatters was founded in 2014 by Simone Coxe, founder of the public relations firm Blanc & Otus, and Chris Boskin, a former member of the National Public Radio and Corporation for Public Broadcasting boards (Doctor 2015). CALmatters is modeled after other state-focused journalism startups such as the *Texas Tribune* (Doctor 2015).

July's additional CALmatters columns fit a profile: authors holding leadership positions in state government, business organizations, or other organized groups advocated for a bill or policy before the California legislature. Of the sixteen non-columnist CALmatters articles published by *The Desert Sun* in July, nine named specific bills in the California Assembly or Senate. CALmatters brought these state debates into the Palm Springs newspaper, informing readers about the positions of nonlocal interest groups and politicians on the action in Sacramento.

Officials advocated for their own bills on their own terms. Senator Holly Mitchell, representing District 30 in Los Angeles, coauthored a CALmatters editorial with Jen Flory, a health policy advocate for the Western Center for Law and Poverty, about Mitchell's bill SB 639, "which would end situations in which patients are signed up for high-interest cards in high-stress medical situations" (Mitchell and Flory 2019). Assemblyman Adam Gray (District 21) wrote for CALmatters that hydropower is "the original source of clean electricity," describing his Assembly Constitutional Amendment (ACA) 17 to recognize hydropower in the state's constitution (Gray 2019). Merced's New Exchequer Dam, located in Gray's district, is not mentioned. This direct advocacy by politicians is informative but serves politicians' interests in sometimes undisclosed ways.

Interest group executives attempted to influence Californians using CALmatters. On July 3, former Assembly Speaker Fabian Nunez wrote a CALmatters op-ed against using cap and trade revenue to fund "pet projects," in his words, such as "clean drinking water, high speed rail, and workforce training" (Nunez 2019). The next day, David Festa, senior Vice President of Ecosystems at Environmental Defense Fund, made the opposing case: the decision to use cap-and-trade money to clean up the Central Valley's contaminated drinking water, "rather than assess a fee on water users or tap into the state's budget surplus," was "cheered by clean water advocates, including my organization, the Environmental Defense Fund" (Festa 2019). This informative debate was useful and civil throughout: Festa's op-ed did not mention Nunez, their stakes in the debate were stated, and both reaffirmed their commitment to conservation.

July's CALmatters op-eds almost followed a template: introduce an issue, talk about a specific bill, praise the bill, and encourage lawmakers to pass it. On Friday, July 5, Robert Jimenez – CEO of Mutual Housing California, a Sacramento-based housing development and advocacy organization – wrote about the hardships of agricultural workers in need of housing, and advocated for passing Assembly Bill (AB) 1783. The bill "would relieve growers from managing the housing by turning that responsibility over to not-for-profit providers," and – conveniently for him – "there are several nonprofits around California that know how to build, manage, and maintain farmworker housing," including "our own Mutual Housing at Spring Lake community in Woodland" (Jimenez 2019). The bill passed the Assembly and awaited a Senate housing committee hearing on Tuesday, July 9, placing his op-ed at a crucial point in the passage timeline. While this organization operates as a nonprofit and advocates about housing-related issues, this CALmatters op-ed. offers their CEO a chance to publicize a bill that helps his business at a critical point in its passage.

For-profit corporations and industry groups also used CALmatters. On July 22, after the University of California (UC) digital library terminated journal renewal negotiations with Dutch academic publisher Elsevier, CALmatters published a critical column from Daniel Marti, head of global public policy at RELX, the parent company of Elsevier. Marti describes UC's position in vague and unflattering terms: the library refused to negotiate, "rejected all offers," and "demanded Elsevier implement a publishing plan that shifts costs to the UC researcher community" (Marti 2019). Elsevier, in Marti's words, "proposed a series of arrangements that would contain costs, achieve the objectives of the Academic Senate, and provide . . . uninterrupted service" (Marti 2019).

On its website, the University of California argues instead that Elsevier tried to restrict open access publishing in high-profile journals (UC Office of Scholarly Communication 2019). No editorial backing UC's position appeared in *The Desert Sun* in the months studied. Other major state university systems, such as the State University of New York, University of North Carolina, and Florida State University broke off their agreements with Elsevier in recent years due to its exorbitant costs (McKenzie 2018), but those are not mentioned either. Marti's editorial is an incomplete picture of the issue, and his affiliation is only noted in his biography at the end. The reliance on CALmatters in July allowed this executive who lives in Washington, DC – the only nonlocal author to appear in *The Desert Sun*'s opinion page in July – to speak unopposed.

Organizations such as CALmatters are an important supplement to the diminishing state house press corps. If they are providing a megaphone for corporate lobbyists to advocate directly to the public unopposed, however, their normative contribution is dubious. Makinen recognized the value of CALmatters content for *The Desert Sun*'s goals of localizing opinion, but was also worried that it could amplify existing disparities: "When you have one opinion editor, no opinion editor, how do we invest the time to elevate those voices that don't come nicely packaged already? It is just a matter of copying and pasting over from a CALmatters server" (Makinen, personal communication, June 18, 2020).

Without partisan cues, voters will use the stances of business and advocacy organizations as a shortcut, or "heuristic," to determine where they stand on complex issues (Lupia 1994). CALmatters articles in July provided readers with these cues about California issues and the stances of political actors who care about those issues. CALmatters op-eds are certainly more informative about the issues facing the state than the national content they replaced. Any change in the media industry has tradeoffs, and state-level syndication services like CALmatters inform Californians about their state government but facilitate outside lobbying by business groups in local newspapers.

3.5 The Promise and Limits of Localization

The Desert Sun successfully removed national politics from its opinion page in July, as Makinen promised, and replaced it with state-level perspectives and local concerns written by non-journalists. Palm Springs residents care about preserving their distinctive arts and architecture, the traffic and transportation issues across the region, and caring for their precarious desert environment. *The Desert Sun* showed that a home style opinion page could happen, but exposed important questions of diversity, privilege, and representation.

Diversity on the opinion page is a complex issue. *New York Times* editorial page editor James Bennet resigned in June 2020 over his handling of an op-ed from Arkansas Senator Tom Cotton proposing a military response to ongoing Black Lives Matter protests (Tracy 2020). Around the same time, "A Letter on Justice and Open Debate," signed by many authors, was published in *Harper's* and advocated for tolerance of differing views (Ackerman et al. 2020). Some believe that tolerance for diverse views is decreasing, while others argue that tolerance for *all* views, including threatening violence against Black Lives Matter protestors or criticizing transgender and LGBTQ rights, prioritizes "open debate" among elites over the safety of oppressed and underrepresented groups and identities (Giorgis 2020).

These disagreements illustrate larger questions about opinion journalism: what does "diversity of opinion" mean? Editors aim for ideological fairness, embrace community concerns, and maintain editorial standards about grammar and style (Hart 2018). An original, provocative, and topically diverse page is more important to editors than one that is representative of gender, race, or ethnicity (Fry 2012). For many editors, that means putting liberal and conservative (or, in the case of national politics, pro-Trump and anti-Trump) perspectives on the page (Page 1996). Both Makinen and Franco were proud that opinion was criticized from both sides: "We get letters. People say we're so incredibly liberal. And then we get people saying, oh, we're not critical enough of Trump and all that stuff" (Makinen, personal communication, June 18, 2020).

While including "both sides" helps meet journalistic standards of objectivity, it can also amplify elite perspectives (Page 1996; Bennett 1990; Gans 1979). Increasingly, activists and younger journalists argue that diversity in reported and opinion journalism means that writers and topics should reflect and respect marginalized perspectives instead of reinforcing dominant systems and voices (Smith 2020).

The opinion page remains white and male, both locally and nationally. Newspapers historically serve as a platform for elite voices and entrenched political interests (Page 1996). There is a "byline gap" in opportunities and hiring (Jacobs and Townsley 2011), as well as submission deficits as high as nine-to-one in favor of submissions by men compared to women (in the *Washington Post*; Fry 2012). Men are also willing to opine on myriad topics, even where they are less than qualified, while women tend to write about their specific expertise (Fry 2012). Less professionalism also does not mean better representation: "More than becoming less white or less male in recent decades, the pundit class has become more diverse only in the sense of becoming less journalist" (Fry 2012).

We were unsure if localization would improve racial, ethnic, and gender diversity. Our results show that a home style opinion page alone may not diversify the pool of writers. If history is any indicator, upending these entrenched hierarchies will require deliberate effort by editors, activists, and organizations (Page 1996). Makinen clearly understood the problem of privilege and access and the effort required to lift up marginalized voices:

> I think people in power are more conscious of how to get access to these platforms, and we need to do a better job of reaching below that tier, the people who not only understand how opinion pages work and are willing to submit to them, and also have PR agencies and PR consultants and stuff who help them craft those messages. (Makinen, personal communication, June 18, 2020)

A newspaper needs to reflect its community to function as a successful public forum. If published debates merely reflect a right–left divide among elites, the newspaper may lose touch with broad segments of its potential readership and customer base. A focus on liberal and conservative perspectives may also encourage more national politics on the op-ed page, polarizing and dividing politically interested readers.

4 Polarization Cools Off in the Desert

When *The Desert Sun* dropped national politics from the opinion page in July 2019, it took a leap of faith that the supply of local content would meet demand. News coverage of partisan conflict creates a vicious cycle: polarization is newsworthy, but coverage of polarization further polarizes readers (Levendusky and Malhotra 2016). *The Desert Sun*'s readers were accustomed to a steady stream of national op-ed columnists, as shown in Section 3. By reducing national political coverage, the July experiment was also intended to reduce polarized rhetoric in the newspaper, with the hopes of having the same effect on readers:

> National columnists would write a lot about Trump and the national political divide. And I felt that was adding to people's unhappiness with the paper, whichever side of it you were on . . . Writing another column about Trump is not going to bring anyone in the community together. (Makinen, personal communication, June 18, 2020)

The July experiment successfully deemphasized political parties on the opinion page. Local politics is generally less partisan than is national politics (Gerber and Hopkins 2011; Trounstine 2009), given the lack of party affiliation in many municipal offices. We expected that explicit mentions of political parties would decrease in July when the focus turned local. A research assistant coded for explicit mentions of Democrats and Republicans (including "GOP"), such as referring to a politician as a party member or describing a proposal as a party's position. We combined those categories into mentions of either major party in the opinion page's op-eds, editorials, or letters (Figure 11).[10]

---

[10] Intercoder agreement was kappa = 1.00 on a random 20 percent subsample.

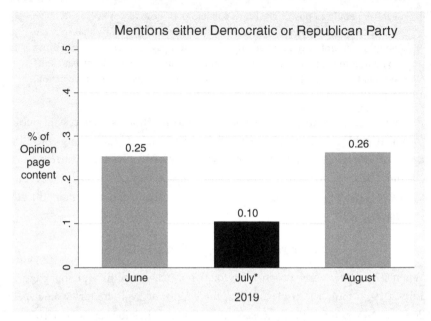

Figure 11 Party mentions on opinion page, by month

Pieces mentioning either Democrats or Republicans fell by more than half in July. In June and August, one in every four opinion page items mentioned one or both of the parties, compared to only one in ten in July. Political topics were less commonly discussed with a partisan frame in *The Desert Sun*, so opinion page readers in July experienced less priming of their partisan, nationalized, political identity than readers of unchanged newspapers.

In today's American politics, partisan identity represents one of the most salient social identities for many individuals (Iyengar and Krupenkin 2018). Deemphasizing partisan identities should slow the growth of affective and social polarization (Iyengar et al. 2019). Did the change in content cool off partisan tensions among *The Desert Sun*'s readers?

In this Section, we use two waves of surveys (conducted at the end of June and late July/early August) in Palm Springs and in Ventura, a comparison community, to test whether the July experiment in home style opinion affected political attitudes. We focus on one of the most important and dangerous trends in American politics today: affective polarization.

Partisan negativity and vitriol roil in contemporary American society. People dislike the opposing party and its members, and feel more socially distant from out-partisans, rating them lower and lower in their esteem (Iyengar et al. 2019). This dislike is increasing in recent decades, particularly since 1990, with no signs of abating (Iyengar et al. 2019; Iyengar and Krupenkin 2018). Affective polarization does not require that opposing partisans' policy preferences are wildly divergent, as with "issue polarization" (Mason 2015): Americans can and do dislike their partisan "enemies" without substantively disagreeing about specific issues (Mason 2018). We focus on affective polarization here as opposed to issue polarization, since deemphasizing partisan identities should be more tightly linked to the emotional and affective elements of polarization than to issues (Iyengar et al. 2019).

Affective polarization influences policy outcomes indirectly, however, since it can lead partisans to devalue bipartisan compromise (Davis 2018). America's federal system all but ensures that one party cannot control all the levers of the federal and state governments simultaneously, meaning that the parties must at least occasionally work together for the government to function. We should not expect elected officials to do the unappealing work of crafting compromise if politically engaged and motivated citizens never reward it.

There are social contours of polarization as well: many would not approve of their child marrying a member of the opposite political party, for example (Mason 2018). Political identity is an easy proxy for religious beliefs, attitudes towards veganism, the Toyota Prius, deer hunting, gun ranges, and even mask-wearing during the 2020/21 COVID-19 pandemic (Pew 2020). Political wins and losses therefore affect many aspects of a person's sense of self (Mason 2018; Davis and Hitt 2017), making venom for the opposite party feel righteous in Americans' minds.[11]

What, if anything, can stem this rising tide of negative partisanship and affective polarization? Nationalized partisan identities, correlated with other social identities, seem to be at the root of the problem. Using the media to deemphasize nationalized partisan identities while priming a cross-cutting local identity could deescalate this cycle of affective polarization (Iyengar et al. 2019).

The Desert Sun did exactly that when it shifted its opinion page focus to local issues: polarization slowed in the areas receiving *The Desert Sun*, compared to those in Ventura who received the unchanged *Ventura County Star*. Affective polarization is a complex and deeply rooted phenomenon, and while these results are encouraging, one single intervention is unlikely to have a large impact. As affective polarization continues to rise in the United States, slowing

---

[11] While there may exist theoretical and empirical limits to the rise of affective polarization, July 2019 featured numerous salient, conflictual, and partisan events that seem unlikely to have slowed or stopped the growth of affective polarization at the national level. Our data in the control community of Ventura bear this dynamic out: the average respondent's level of affective polarization rose during this month, even without a maximally activating event like an election taking place. Nevertheless, it would be desirable to replicate this research in a different community during an election month in the future.

this increase might be the most that scholars could plausibly expect to detect (Iyengar et al. 2019). While a home style opinion page could not halt polarization, it slowed noticeably in Palm Springs compared to Ventura.

4.1 Research and Survey Design: Palm Springs and Ventura

We study Palm Springs, California for one reason: while every local newspaper in America in July of 2019 could have deemphasized national politics on its opinion page, only *The Desert Sun* actually did so, for the reasons as outlined in Makinen's column. As such, the opinion page changes made by *The Desert Sun* provided a natural experiment (Cook and Campbell 1979). For several decades now, social and political scientists have recognized the vital importance of carefully identifying causal effects (King 1991) as opposed to potentially spurious correlations in observational data. Scholars leverage various experimental methods – primarily laboratory, field, and natural experiments – to carry out this work (McDermott 2002).

Although our experiment occurred in the real world, giving our study excellent "external validity," we do not actually control assignment to treatment and therefore have to make some adjustments to the design. Without random or as-if random assignment of a treatment, it is difficult to know whether, in a particular geographic, temporal, and political context, a newspaper's decision to emphasize local issues over national politics in their opinion section *caused* changes in the attitudes of the community they serve. For example, if Palm Springs is unusually educated or bipartisan, we would not know if the change in the opinion page itself were actually causing changes in community attitudes, or if the change were simply prompted by the characteristics of the community to begin with. Thus, our analysis also requires a comparison community: if we only studied the community served by *The Desert Sun*, we leave ourselves vulnerable to the possibility that polarization slowed everywhere in July 2019.[12]

We deal with this challenge methodologically by combining our analysis of a natural experiment with a powerful causal inference technique: a difference-in-differences design (Abadie 2005; Card and Krueger 1993). We measure the quantities of interest in two statistically similar populations before some change

---

[12] In spite of the fact that our experiment occurred naturally in the sense that the manipulation of the treatment was not under our control, it does not meet the criteria for a true natural experiment. The adjustments we made allow comparison across treatment and control communities, but the assignment was not random or as good as random (Dunning 2012). The situation dictated that we select a comparison community to serve as our control, and our selection was purposive based on matching on observable characteristics. Our study is quasi-experimental, with nonequivalent-groups (Trochim, Donnelly and Arora 2016), which we analyze with difference in differences for the reasons outlined above.

or intervention, for example, *The Desert Sun's* natural experiment, then measure the same populations after the treatment. Both populations may change in this time period, but the difference in *how and how much* the treated and control communities changed represents the causal effect of the experiment. This design mitigates against the possibility that observed changes in our treated community were caused by something else happening at the same time across many areas, including but not limited to our treated area.

We compare changes from Wave 1 to Wave 2 of our survey in Palm Springs, which received the "treatment" of dropping national politics in July, to changes from Wave 1 to Wave 2 surveys in Ventura, California, where the *Ventura County Star* did not change its opinion page. This analytical approach is akin to a difference-in-differences analysis using repeated cross-sectional data.

The experiment conducted by *The Desert Sun* in July allows us a rare opportunity to rigorously identify causal effects in the real world. Most studies of media effects, including our analyses regarding news use and knowledge in Section 2, cannot isolate a causal effect or else sacrifice real-world relevance by using a laboratory setting. Without evidence of a *causal* effect of this editorial change, editors and publishers should exercise caution before conducting a similar experiment themselves.

Ventura is roughly sixty-eight miles northwest of Los Angeles, while Palm Springs is approximately 106 miles southeast. Figure 12 shows the circulation regions of both papers. They do not share television media markets, and there is no overlap in their circulation areas. Palm Springs (population 44,540) is smaller than Ventura (population 111,128), but demographically, the two cities have comparable populations (U.S. Census Bureau 2019).

Palm Springs is 83.3 percent white, with 27.8 percent Hispanic identifiers; Ventura is 84.4 percent white but slightly more Hispanic at 36.4 percent. Neither has a large Black population, at 3.7 percent and 1.8 percent, respectively. Palm Springs respondents are statistically older by about two and a half years on average, wealthier, and less educated, but Ventura and Palm Springs respondents are statistically indistinguishable on other important variables such party ID, ideology, preference for the local newspaper, political knowledge, and political involvement.[13] Although there are some differences in the populations, the newspapers that serve these communities are both owned by Gannett and have roughly similar circulations.

These similarities matter because our difference-in-differences design assumes that if Palm Springs were never treated with the editorial change, then its

---

[13] These comparisons derive from nonparametric Kolmogorov-Smirnov comparison of distribution tests conducted in Stata 15.1 using the ksmirnov command. Full results found in Table 4.B1 of the Appendix.

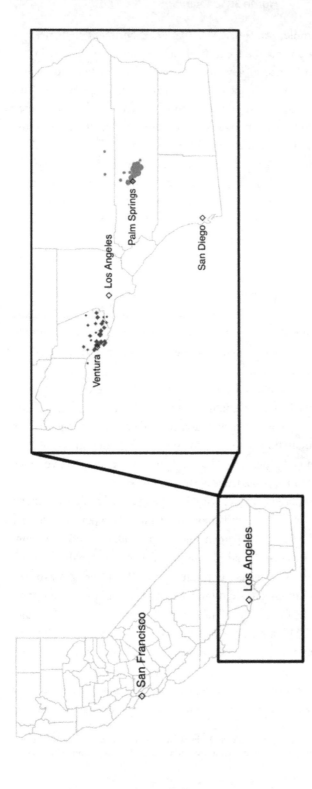

Figure 12 Circulation areas of *The Desert Sun* (light gray) and the *Ventura County Star* (dark gray). Dot size corresponds to circulation in each ZIP code. Tables of circulation by ZIP code can be found in Tables 4.A1 (Palm Springs) and 4.A2 (Ventura) in the Appendix. Data from the Alliance for Audited Media's Media Intelligence Center

trajectory in terms of polarization would be the same as Ventura's. To make that assumption plausible, the two communities must be as similar as possible with regard to any variables that might otherwise impact the outcomes we study (Dunning 2008). We considered a number of candidate communities in California before concluding that Ventura was our best available match.

We discovered *The Desert Sun*'s July experiment on June 8, 2019, contacted Qualtrics on June 11, and were approved by the IRB at Louisiana State University on June 21. Qualtrics was chosen because it could reliably locate respondents in the circulation areas for *The Desert Sun* of Palm Springs and the *Ventura County Star* of Ventura on short notice. Circulation ZIP codes were obtained from the Alliance for Audited Media's Media Intelligence Center. *The Desert Sun* circulates in sixteen ZIP codes, with a total circulation of 26,406, and the *Ventura County Star* circulates in twenty-seven ZIP codes with a total circulation of 30,088. Full ZIP codes, with circulation by ZIP, can be found in Table 4.A1 in the Appendix.

The first wave of the Qualtrics survey was fielded from June 21 through June 30, to avoid contamination with the beginning of the treatment period on July 1. Qualtrics applied a series of age, location, and engagement restrictions (time spent on questions) to discover quality respondents who were over eighteen and lived in the given ZIP codes.[14] Respondents entered their ZIP code, and if their ZIP code did not match those in which *The Desert Sun* or the *Ventura County Star* circulate (respectively for each survey), their survey was ended. Qualtrics also included safeguards against respondents rushing through the surveys: those who completed multiple-question batteries in less than one second were deemed "speeders," and their survey was ended. The reader surveys were identical to the Qualtrics surveys but did not contain the ZIP code restrictions or the timing restrictions.

The surveys in Wave 1 and Wave 2 were nearly identical in Palm Springs and Ventura. Wave 1 of the Qualtrics surveys contained 422 responses in Palm Springs and 525 responses in Ventura. Wave 2 contained 525 respondents in each survey location. Other than several questions at the end of the Wave 2 surveys about newspaper use,[15] the survey waves are identical within cities and comparable without priming respondents to think about the treatment before answering variables of interest. In the interest of brevity, the following sections will only include descriptions of the variables relevant to our models and hypotheses on affective polarization. The full text of Wave 1 Qualtrics surveys in Ventura and Palm Springs are provided in Appendix 4.C.

---

[14] The age question, asked immediately following the consent form, asked "What is your year of birth?" If respondents answered with a year later than 2001, their survey was ended.

[15] These questions were requested by *The Desert Sun*'s editors, and we were happy to oblige.

4.1.1 Preregistered Hypotheses: Affective and Social Polarization

Before we received Wave 2 of the data, we preregistered hypotheses with the Open Science Foundation. Preregistration of our hypotheses ensures that the results we report are not based on any post hoc adjustments to our data analysis plan that could otherwise manipulate the statistical significance of our results (Nosek et al. 2015; Gelman and Loken 2014). As such, the results represent analytical choices we committed to before we possessed any real data. We strongly endorse preregistration as a tool to enhance the credibility of social science research. Table 2 lists all the preregistered hypotheses and results that we discuss in this chapter.

We expect that a newspaper's shift in focus to local news will lower affective and social polarization, as partisan exemplars in the media will be closer to home and exposure to polarizing national rhetoric should decrease. This

Table 2 Preregistered hypotheses and results. "Supported" indicates statistical significance at the level of alpha = 0.05

Hypothesis	Result
H1a: Treatment decreases affective polarization.	Not Supported
H1b: Treatment decreases social polarization.	Not Supported
H2a: Those with a preference for local newspaper and received the treatment will be relatively less affectively polarized post-treatment than those who did not receive treatment.	Supported
H2b: Those with a preference for local newspaper and received the treatment will be relatively less socially polarized post-treatment than those who did not receive treatment.	Supported
H3a: Those with more national political knowledge and received the treatment will be relatively less affectively polarized post-treatment than those who did not receive treatment.	Supported
H3b: Those with more national political knowledge and received the treatment will be relatively less socially polarized post-treatment than those who did not receive treatment.	Supported
H4a: Those who participate more in politics who received the treatment will be relatively less affectively polarized post-treatment than those who did not receive treatment.	Supported
H4b: Those who participate more in politics and received the treatment will be relatively less socially polarized post-treatment than those who did not receive treatment.	Supported

hypothesis – that the change in affective polarization will be lower for Palm Springs-area respondents than for Ventura respondents – serves as the basis for our subsequent analyses of moderating variables.

Measuring affective polarization requires a respondent's party affiliation and their ratings of various politicians and parties. We assessed partisanship using the standard seven-point party identification battery: respondents were asked if they thought of themselves as Republican, Democrat, independent, libertarian, or other (with a text entry box), then directed them to a strength of party identification question if they identified as Democrat or Republican, or a question about their partisan lean if they gave any answer other than Democrat or Republican to the first question. These answers were combined to form a seven-point Likert scale of partisan identification, from strong Democrat (1) to strong Republican (7).

We measure affective polarization using feeling thermometers (Lelkes et al., 2017; Iyengar et al., 2012). In the first, we ask respondents: "Rate how you feel towards these groups on a scale of 0 to 100. Zero means very unfavorable and 100 means very favorable. Fifty means you do not feel favorable or unfavorable. How would you rate your feelings towards each of these?" The groups they were asked to evaluate included: Democrats, Republicans, immigrants, politicians, Muslims, and Evangelical Christians. In the second, we asked respondents to "rate feelings towards politicians on a scale of 0 to 100."[16] Some state and national politicians were included in both surveys, such as President Donald Trump; Speaker of the House Nancy Pelosi; California Governor Gavin Newsom; and California Senator Dianne Feinstein. In Palm Springs, respondents were asked about "Raul Ruiz (Palm Springs area Congressman)" and "Robert Moon (Palm Springs Mayor)," while Ventura residents were asked about "Julia Brownley (Ventura County Congresswoman" and "Katie Hill (Ventura County Congresswoman)." The dependent variable used in the analyses is constructed from only the thermometers for Democrats and Republicans.

We also measure social polarization. When people identify more strongly with their partisan group, they are biased against opposing partisans, take actions to defend their party, and feel angrier about threats to the group (Mason 2018). Social polarization occurs when polarized partisan fighting in national politics spills over into social strife, affecting even non-elite opposing partisans in social situations with consequences in actions and prejudices beyond simply disliking the out-party more as affective polarization describes (Iyengar et al. 2019).

---

[16] The scale was described to respondents as follows: "Zero means very unfavorable and 100 means very favorable. Fifty means you do not feel favorable or unfavorable."

We measure social polarization by asking, "How do you think you would react if a member of your immediate family told you they were going to marry a [out-party member]?" (Mason 2018). We group responses into a binary variable: subjects answering "Unhappy" were coded as 1, while those answering "Wouldn't matter at all" or "Happy" were coded as 0.

We expected that any effects on affective and social polarization might be conditional on factors that indicate political involvement and exposure to treatment. These hypotheses share the same dependent variables – the difference between in-party and out-party feeling thermometer ratings (affective) and reaction to a child marrying an out-party partisan (social).

All moderating variables are measured pretreatment, during Wave 1. These moderators speak to potential causal mechanisms for a relative change in affective and social polarization: exposure to the local newspaper; political knowledge; and political participation.

4.1.2 Moderators: Local News Preference, Political Knowledge, and Political Participation

While the institutional presence or absence of a newspaper does seem to cause some aggregate effects in a geographic area, it stands to reason that actual exposure to the op-ed page of *The Desert Sun* would cause a greater change in affective polarization (Coppock et al. 2018). As such, people who prefer to get their news from a local newspaper should be likelier to exhibit a treatment effect. The more engaged and knowledgeable citizens should be most likely to detect changes in political media coverage, making it more likely that aggregate changes to affective polarization will likely be found in this group (Hitt, Saunders, and Scott 2019). We will first compare news preferences in Palm Springs and Ventura in Wave 1 surveys, in order to assess their local news preferences before the experiment and provide a baseline for understanding people in southern California view local news.

Preferring the Local Newspaper

We first asked how closely respondents followed news about four places – international, national, local, and "your neighborhood" – on a three-point scale from "Not at all closely" to "Very closely." Of these types of news, international news was lowest (mean = 1.96), while local news was highest (mean = 2.29), across both Palm Springs and Ventura.

Next, we asked which medium respondents preferred for local news and information. The newspaper preference variable used in our analyses was created from this question but made dichotomous: prefers newspaper (1) or prefers another source (0). The options in the survey were: reading a local print newspaper, local radio station, local television station, a social media site such as Facebook, YouTube, or Snapchat, or another local news source. Each of these source options included "or its news website or app." Figure 13 shows these results.

While Palm Springs and Ventura respondents used newspapers at similar rates (24.9 percent vs. 23.2 percent), there are large differences in television and social media use. Palm Springs residents are much more likely to prefer television news (44.5 percent vs. 36 percent), but much less likely to prefer social media (13.7 percent vs. 22.1 percent). A possible explanation: Palm Springs is its own television media market while Ventura lies at the far edge of the second-largest market in the nation, Los Angeles. Palm Springs' local television news is more "local" than Ventura's, by definition, which might make it more appealing. Interestingly, the tradeoff for media use is with social media, not newspapers.

After reporting which medium they used, respondents were asked a series of questions about why they chose to consume news at all, on a three-point scale from "Not at all important" to "Important." These options encompass a range of possible reasons to consume news, from social reasons ("Helps me talk to my friends, family, and colleagues about what's going on in the news") to practical ("Helps me find places to go and things to do," "Helps me care for myself or my family," "Is enjoyable or entertaining,"), civic ("Helps me stay informed to be a better citizen," "Shares my point of view," "Helps me decide where I stand on things"), and quality ("Is very good at covering an issue or topic I care a lot about").

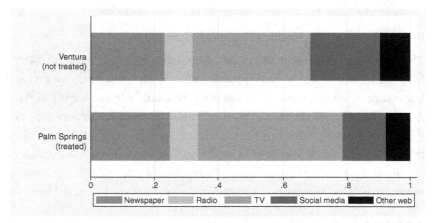

Figure 13 Local media preferences in Palm Springs and Ventura, Wave 1

Across both communities, the most important reason to use news was to stay informed (M = 2.52). After that, people wanted news to be good at covering an issue they care about (M = 2.39). Most of the rest of the issues were clustered just above a value of 2 ("Somewhat important"), with by far the lowest rated reason being "Shares my point of view" (M = 1.85). People are not looking for ideologically congenial information when reading news, or at least do not want to express that in a poll: instead, people want to stay informed and care for their families (M = 2.19).

The next set of questions assessed the perceived influence and connections between local news and the community it serves. First, we asked whether local news has "a lot of influence" (1) or "not much of an influence" (0) on the respondent's community, followed by a question asking whether "Overall, would you say that local journalists are mostly in touch or out of touch with your local community?" There were significant differences between Ventura and Palm Springs on these factors: compared to the *Ventura County Star, The Desert Sun* was perceived as more in touch (0.78 vs 0.7; p = 0.004) and more influential (0.59 vs. 0.51; p = 0.014). Palm Springs residents may view their newspaper more favorably than do Ventura residents.

These questions provide insight into the attitudes of Palm Springs and Ventura residents towards their local news, the reasons they use it, and their preferred media sources. For the purposes of the analyses, we will only look at those who choose the newspaper. Attitudes are mostly similar, although *The Desert Sun* seems to be more influential within its community. Newspaper use is similar across communities, although television is more popular in Palm Springs while Ventura residents use social media more. Since the natural experiment we analyze concerns newspapers, the similarity between communities is reassuring.

National Political Knowledge

The next section of questions addresses the political knowledge of respondents. Media use and political knowledge tend to be closely associated, but political knowledge is almost always measured using nationally relevant questions about the three branches of the federal government.[17] The most commonly used and demonstrably predictive set of questions is the five-question battery suggested by Delli Carpini and Keeter (1997), which asks respondents to identify the vice president; the branch of government responsible for determining the constitutionality of laws; the party currently in majority control of the House of

---

[17] We do not include a hypothesis for local political knowledge, given the dearth of theory about its relationship to national political knowledge.

Representatives; the majority required in the House and Senate to override a presidential veto; and whether Democrats or Republicans are more conservative at a national level. In our data, residents of Ventura got an average of 3.37 questions right, while residents of Palm Springs got an average of 3.30 questions right, a nonsignificant difference.

While there are concerns about knowledge measures in online surveys (Clifford and Jerit 2016), knowledge assesses attentiveness and political awareness, which has important links to media use and preferences. There is a tension inherent to the study of political attentiveness and media effects. On one hand, those paying attention to media should logically be most affected by its content. On the other hand, those most attentive to media tend to have strong partisan attitudes that are the most difficult to change (Zaller 1992). Either way, knowledge is an important moderator of media effects and deserves inclusion in our analyses.

Political Participation

Many Americans dislike politics altogether, but dislike for the other party is more commonly found in strong partisans (Kinder and Kalmoe 2018; Klar et al. 2018). However, those same strong partisans are also most likely to participate in politics (Delli Carpini and Keeter 1997). These tendencies are exacerbated by America's partisan and nationalizing political media (Hopkins 2018). The two major political parties carefully cultivate a national brand, leading to consistent partisan voting patterns across all levels of American elections (Darr, Hitt, and Dunaway 2018; Davis and Dunaway 2016; Davis and Mason 2016).

The questions about out-party attitudes were interrupted by a standard question on political involvement, in which respondents were asked to select all of the political activities they participated in over the past year: rally attendance, working for a party or candidate, active group membership, contacting elected officials, donating money to candidates or groups, displaying a bumper sticker or button, and publicly supporting a campaign on social media. In our survey data, residents of Ventura reported an average of 1.28 such activities (SD = 1.29). Residents of Palm Springs reported an average of 1.45 such activities (SD = 1.41). The large standard deviations show substantial variation in the political activities of residents within these communities.

4.2 Results: Polarization Slows (For Some) In Palm Springs

We do not find unconditional support for our first hypotheses listed in Table 2. The treatment did not cause a statistically meaningful change in social polarization in aggregate in the treated area. Surprisingly, we find an unconditional and positive, statistically significant relationship between the treatment and affective polarization. This relationship is in the opposite direction of our preregistered hypothesis. Given the national political climate in July of 2019, it is sensible that affective polarization might be on the rise generally, and Palm Springs is not necessarily an exception. Expecting that *The Desert Sun's* experiment could stop polarization in its tracks for an entire community is perhaps asking too much of a single media outlet. Full regression results are presented in Table 4.B2 of the Appendix.

The kinds of people who prefer to read the newspaper, know politics well, and participate in it regularly might be more likely to change their attitudes than the general population. We find statistically significant support for our conditional hypotheses: a preference for the local newspaper (H2a and H2b), national political knowledge (H3a and H3b), and political involvement (H4a and H4b), all moderate the effect of the treatment in the hypothesized direction. Figures 14 and 15 present these results graphically for affective and social polarization respectively.[18]

Panel (a) of Figure 14 shows that those who prefer the newspaper in Palm Springs were steady with regard to affective polarization. In Ventura, those who preferred the paper for their news reported an increase in their antipathy towards their opposite party. Our model predicts that residents of Ventura who prefer getting their news from the local newspaper increased their social polarization by about five points (on a one-hundred-point scale) in the month of July. Residents of Palm Springs who prefer the newspaper increased on this scale by only one point.

Panel (b) of Figure 14 shows similar shifts among the politically knowledgeable: relative to residents of Ventura, the differences in affective polarization between the more and less knowledgeable were slightly ameliorated in Palm Springs. The difference in the relative predicted change in affective polarization is very modest: affective polarization among the knowledgeable in Ventura is predicted to have risen by 3.56 points on a one-hundred-point scale, relative to a 3.29 point increase among the politically knowledgeable in Palm Springs. However, the coefficient on the interaction (after treatment, in Palm Springs, high political knowledge), as presented in Table 4.B3 of the Appendix, is negative and significant (-8.72; $p = 0.027$). While not a large difference between communities, polarization among the politically knowledgeable was significantly slowed in Palm Springs compared to Ventura.

Panel (c) tells a similar story: in the treated community of Palm Springs, the politically involved did not lower their reported levels of affective or social

---

[18] We include graphs with error bars in Figures 4.B1 and 4.B2 of the Appendix.

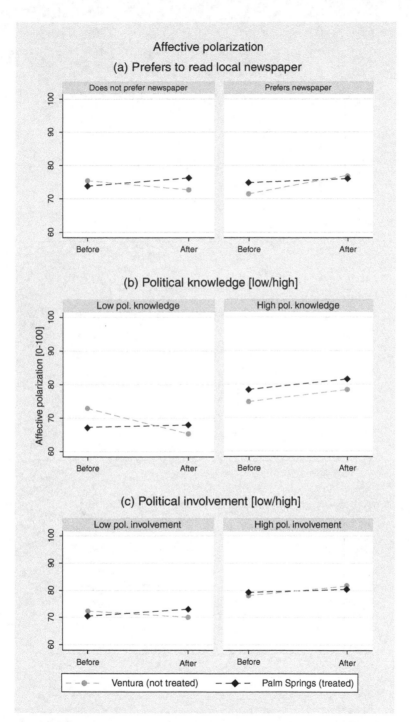

Figure 14 Changes in affective polarization before and after July in Palm Springs and Ventura among those who (a) do and do not prefer the newspaper to receive local news; (b) have high or low levels of national political knowledge; and (c) participate in politics at high or low rates. Full results in Table 4.B3 of the Appendix

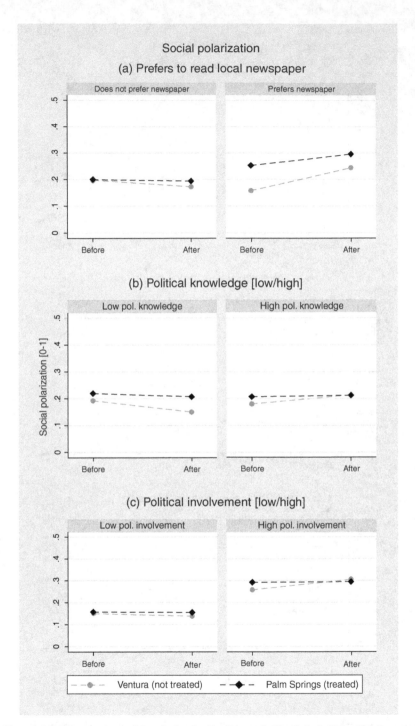

Figure 15 Changes in social polarization before and after July in Palm Springs and Ventura among those who (a) do and do not prefer the newspaper to receive local news; (b) have high or low levels of national political knowledge; and (c) participate in politics at high or low rates. Full results in Table 4.B3 of the Appendix

polarization. Rather, the gap between the more and less involved narrowed relative to the untreated community of Ventura. Substantively speaking, our model estimates that affective polarization rose among the politically involved in Ventura by about four points on a one-hundred-point scale in July, compared to only one point in Palm Springs.

Figure 15 shows that *The Desert Sun's* experiment influenced social polarization to an even greater degree. Panel (a) of Figure 15 shows that residents of Ventura who prefer the newspaper increased the probability that they would report being uncomfortable with a child marrying a member of the out-party from 0.16 to 0.24 in the month of July. In Palm Springs, however, residents who prefer the newspaper increased this same predicted probability by less, from 0.25 to 0.30.[19] The divergent changes in affective and social polarization across our two communities, while positive in all cases, show how *The Desert Sun* Opinion page experiment slowed polarization in Palm Springs.

In Panel (b), we see similar and slightly larger relative increases across the politically knowledgeable for social polarization. Our model estimates that a knowledgeable resident of Ventura increased their probability of social polarization from 0.18 to 0.21 in July. The same probability remained at 0.21 in Palm Springs before and after *The Desert Sun*'s experiment. Knowledge was a stronger moderator of social polarization than affective polarization, where there was little substantive difference in changes between the communities measured.

Panel (c) shows that political participation also moderated the effect on social polarization. The predicted probability that a politically involved resident of Ventura gives a socially polarized response rose from 0.26 to 0.31 over the month of July, while the predicted probability of Palm Springs residents giving the socially polarized response rose only from 0.29 to 0.30.

Taken together, these results corroborate the claim of Iyengar et al. (2019): affective polarization is tough to change, and large shifts in this metric are unlikely. It would strain the bounds of credulity if we observed dramatic decreases in affective polarization in Palm Springs as a function of a one-month experiment by a single news source, especially when limited to the opinion page. However, we observe a consistent pattern across our three conditional models: in each case, affective and social polarization rise less in

---

[19] All marginal effects calculated using the margins command in Stata 15.1. Index variables set at the mean for continuous variables and the mode for discrete variables.

the treated Palm Springs community. This dynamic demonstrates that local newspapers can slow polarization by adjusting the focus of their opinion page.

4.3 Slowing a Rising Tide

Utilizing a before and after survey design and difference-in-differences analysis, we observed little change in affective or social polarization among the very Palm Springs citizens who might be expected to pay the most attention to the political content of their local paper: the politically knowledgeable, the politically active, and those who prefer the paper as their news source. A corresponding set of attentive, knowledgeable, and active citizens in similar (but untreated) Ventura County, California, showed consistently larger increases in social and affective polarization over the same month. *The Desert Sun*'s re-localization experiment counterbalanced the impact of hyper-partisan national political news and briefly slowed the rising tide of affective polarization. These findings are more evidence that priming cross-cutting nonpartisan identities, such as membership in a geographic community, reduces affective polarization (Iyengar et al. 2019).

Changes to the media environment may simply avoid fanning the flames of affective and social polarization even further, as we find in Palm Springs. Given that newspaper op-eds powerfully shape public opinion about contemporary salient political issues, among both elites and the mass public, and this op-ed effect does not appear to be conditional on party affiliation (Coppock et al. 2018), it is reasonable that the opinion page could exert such influence over a community.

These results suggest a possible path forward for local journalists who are concerned about American politics. Emphasizing local issues and shared nonpartisan identities slows polarization for the most engaged and knowledgeable readers. If editorial decisions such as going local-only can have these effects, it is even more essential to retain and support local newspapers. The civic benefits of local news depend on it (Darr, Hitt, and Dunaway 2018).

There is an unavoidable tradeoff between precise causal inference and broader generalizability when conducting experimental research. By studying two California counties with a difference-in-differences design, we carefully identify the impact of *The Desert Sun*'s re-localization of its op-ed page. The home styles of newspapers and what resonates with their readers are very different across the United States, however. We hope these results encourage more news outlets to undertake experiments in localization so that the generalizability of these findings can continue to be studied in a natural context.

5 The Future of the Opinion Page

Since July 2019, the crisis in local news arguably worsened (Abernathy 2020). Gatehouse Media acquired the *The Desert Sun*'s owner, Gannett, just after the July experiment ended (Edmonds 2019). The COVID-19 pandemic spotlighted the need for local news and the perils facing the industry: visits to local news sites increased 89 percent from February to March 2020 (Frank 2020), but advertising revenue declined sharply. Several newspapers, such as the *Waterbury Record* (VT), *Daily Clintonian* (IN), and *Eden Prairie News* (MN), closed for good (Hare 2020). Gannett newspapers furloughed employees for one week every month in 2020 and laid off many reporters and editors (Hare and LaForme 2020), including *The Desert Sun*'s statehouse reporter, Gabrielle Canon, who was hired in July 2019 (Canon 2020; Makinen 2019b).

Cuts to editor positions make it tougher to maintain opinion pages in the surviving newspapers: "The unspoken crisis in local journalism is the gutting of editor ranks" (Makinen, personal communication, June 18, 2020). Without an editor, it is more difficult to solicit and edit op-eds from the community (Enda 2013). Julie Makinen, Editor of *The Desert Sun*, repeatedly emphasized the importance of employing an opinion editor: "Investing even in a part-time opinion editor for local I think could pay huge dividends in terms of community relations, but also just bringing more local content to places. And all you have to pay for is the editor" (Makinen, personal communication, June 18, 2020).

The opinion pages of American newspapers stand at a historical crossroads. Publishing opinion journalism can make newspapers appear biased (Kahn and Kenney 2002) and confuse readers: for example, only 43 percent of people say that they can easily distinguish news from opinion in online news and social media (Loker 2019). While this perception could make editorials and opinion seem troublesome for newspapers (Rosenberg 2020), our results show that a home style opinion page can help calm partisan tensions.

In this concluding Section, we make recommendations based on our findings that eliminating national politics on an opinion page slows polarization while amplifying local issues. We propose that philanthropists and newspaper owners prioritize training and supporting opinion editors. Broader investment in state services such as CALmatters would help opinion pages localize, although they are susceptible to influence by elites with access to public relations professionals. Finally, we suggest reinvigorating professional associations, which could distribute trainings and best practices to opinion editors, particularly regarding diversity and representation. July's national news hiatus experiment was well-received by employees, ownership, and consumers. At a time when the value of opinion content is being questioned, emphasizing home style and excluding national politics could be a good option for editors, owners, and philanthropists looking to strengthen their contribution to their communities and to democracy.

5.1 The Benefits of Localizing Opinion

Local newspapers with sufficient resources should focus their opinion page on mostly, if not entirely, topics below the level of national politics. Regardless of the normative democratic benefits to their readership, a newspaper cannot be expected to adopt a change if it is overly difficult, opposed by ownership, or unpopular with readership. *The Desert Sun*'s experiment showed that localizing the opinion page is popular and worth the investment.

Makinen described the opinion page as essential to community journalism, which she defined as "the value proposition of presenting content that is very specific to a geographic area in which our product is distributed and consumed and has specific relevancy for the people who live and work in these places" (Makinen, personal communication, June 18, 2020). Editors such as Makinen want to maintain localism despite falling revenues and staff cuts, and an opinion page can bring more community voices into the newspaper and re-center local topics at a low cost:

> A lot of local news has been hollowed out due to corporate ownership and . . .
> business model challenges of local news over the last twenty years. We've
> seen increasing trends toward stuffing papers full of AP content, national
> content, stuff that is sort of off the shelf and can be produced from anywhere,
> to the point now where you have newspapers that are . . . ghost newspapers or
> zombie newspapers. Besides the limited amount of reporting we can do with
> the staff we have locally, opinion content is one of the, I think, remaining
> pillars of local content and discussion. And the best part is that there's not
> a lot of cost to it. It's pretty low . . . It's free, in general. But you need an editor
> to manage it. (Makinen, personal communication, June 18, 2020)

Cost is an essential concern, particularly as revenue issues lead local newspapers to outsource their content or change their definitions of "local" (Usher 2019), and low-quality local news reporting often follows these changes. By investing in opinion editors, newspapers might be able to continue to amplify local voices and issues even as reporting resources dwindle.

Both Franco and Makinen considered the local-only experiment a success with a lasting legacy in the newspaper and community. The recruitment and encouragement of contributors by the editors in July 2019, while more difficult in the short term, helped build an enduring pool of local writers that continued their relationship with the newspaper:

> Some of the readers who read the opinion page but had never contributed, that
> spurred them to contribute. And once you write a letter or submit a column,
> the first one's always the toughest . . . I saw names during July that I hadn't

seen before and I've seen them since. And that's a good thing because it's supposed to be a conversation and it's supposed to be communal; it's not supposed to be the same ten people or twelve people or thirty people. (Franco, personal communication, June 18, 2020)

As opinion editor, Franco's job is easier when more local writers want to contribute: regular submissions from locals help him fill the opinion page with reliable content. Letters to the editor and op-ed submissions represent voices that might otherwise not be heard, "creating and sustaining a culture of argument at the grassroots level" (Hart 2018). If localizing the opinion page stimulates more submissions and engages local organizations, it is worthwhile for local newspapers.

   Gannett, the newspaper's parent company, also approved of the experiment according to Makinen. The project happened at a critical time for the chain's stance towards its opinion pages:

> [Gannett] know(s) about it. The feedback I got was really positive. There's been a larger conversation in Gannett about opinion content, whether to continue it . . . Opinion content does not generally pull in huge page views. And so there's been philosophical debate in company about whether . . . they should continue investing in it. And obviously, some markets have made the decision to eliminate the whole opinion editor and have really kind of walked away from it. (Makinen, personal communication, June 18, 2020)

Some Gannett newspapers are investing in opinion pages while others are eliminating editorial staff, making the future of the op-ed page genuinely uncertain (Loker 2019). As Makinen referenced, another Gannett newspaper, the *Providence Journal* (RI), recently stopped writing editorials altogether (Rosenberg 2020). The editor said the decision was to reduce the appearance of bias, but budget cuts seem more likely: the *Journal* laid off its editorial page editor, former Pulitzer Prize finalist Edward Achorn, one week prior to the announcement (Achorn 2020; Benton 2020). Other Gannett newspapers are innovating rather than shutting down the op-ed page: in Nashville, *The Tennessean* implemented a year-long project focused on civility in 2017 (Plazas 2019; Hart 2018), while Milwaukee's *Journal Sentinel* replaced opinion journalism with an "Ideas Lab" focused on "solutions journalism" exploring policy solutions to pressing community problems (Haynes 2019).

   The Desert Sun's readers generally enjoyed the localized opinion page in July, and several readers sent letters to express that. Readers' letters in June called the upcoming experiment "a splendid decision" and "a stroke of genius," expressing hope that "it will catch on and become a permanent thing" (June 13, Semes 2019; June 13, Spencer 2019). Others felt the editor's decision was "disappointing" as it "muted" and "censored" readers and denied them the chance to criticize Trump's policies (June 13, Winet and Winet 2019; June 23, Malacoff 2019). Later feedback included criticism of Makinen's "mandate" (July 4, Morrison 2019) as well as praise from this reader in Alameda: "I intend to suggest it to our local paper and hope it results in a more coherent and collaborative dialogue in my community and yours" (July 13, Rude 2019).

In our reader-distributed surveys, 23 percent liked the local focus and 5 percent did not, but only 38 percent of respondents were aware of the change and 71 percent reported having no opinion. Comments in the online survey echoed these results: "I appreciate that it was actually relevant to the community," and "I love it! I can get national news anywhere. Local reporting is so important!" Even those with gripes about the newspaper, or who were unaware, were positive: "Didn't know that. I applaud the decision," and "Better but biased."

The Desert Sun showed that localizing the opinion page can engage readers and recruit writers while chilling polarization. The short-term investment deepened the pool of regular local contributors. The readers who noticed the change largely approved, and ownership was supportive. Newspapers should adopt this localization policy because it is popular, cost-effective in the long run, and engages community groups as stakeholders in the newspaper.

5.2 Investing in Opinion

As opinion editor positions become imperiled by budget cuts, more philanthropic dollars should be given to supporting, hiring, and retaining those staffers. If philanthropists invested in opinion page editors, encouraged localization, and demonstrated similar positive effects, ownership groups might be likelier to hire and retain opinion editors at this precarious time.

Journalism philanthropy quadrupled in the last decade, with $1.7 billion in journalism-related grants given out between 2009 and 2019 (Armour-Jones 2019), including investigative journalism ($326 million), advocacy journalism ($185 million), and citizen journalism ($42 million). Philanthropists have largely focused on news at the expense of opinion, which is ripe for investment and assistance. Kevin Loker, Director of Program Operations and Partnerships at the American Press Institute (API), confirmed this in an interview:

> There are a lot of efforts from associations, and support groups, and funders that want more engagement in the news side, in the news product part, in the reporting part … [but] opinion sections feel like a natural place for real engagement that serves a lot of the goals of those movements in journalism right now. (Loker, personal communication, June 29, 2020)

We recommend that these organizations consider funding or subsidizing full or part-time opinion editor positions and encourage those editors to localize their pages. This approach could provide a more efficient and effective impact for benefactors' investments, giving local groups new and prominent platforms while providing appealing civic benefits in the community.

State-level services such as CALmatters make it easier for local newspapers to provide information on state government and should be created and supported in more states. CALmatters already receives support from the Knight Foundation, which recently funded its improved content management system (Schmidt 2019). Of its $3.5 million in revenue in 2018, 75 percent came from individual major donors, leaving room for growth for donations from philanthropic organizations. In 2019, eleven state-level nonprofit news services such as *VTDigger* (Vermont), the *Connecticut Mirror, Mississippi Today*, and Wyoming's *WyoFile*, received grant support from the American Journalism Project (Schmidt 2019), which is funded by a network of philanthropists including the Knight Foundation, Democracy Fund, Craig Newmark Philanthropies, and Facebook Journalism Project.

Donors should support training and recruitment of opinion writers from underrepresented groups. There are few organizations devoted to op-ed coaching and support, and more should exist at the state level. One national organization, the OpEd Project, trains and recruits writers from underrepresented communities, connects them with media mentors, and distributes their ideas to media gatekeepers (The OpEd Project 2020). If this model were implemented locally, representation would improve on local opinion pages.

More professional support is needed for opinion journalists and editors. The Association of Opinion Journalists shrank by 55 percent from 2006 to 2013 before falling below 200 members and being absorbed by the American Society of News Editors in 2017 (ASNE 2017; Enda 2013). The ASNE promised to maintain web resources for opinion journalists (ASNE 2017), but when the organization merged with Associated Press Media Editors and renamed the News Leaders Association (NLA), it did not survive the transition. As of July 2020, the old website still exists but is unchanged since 2018.

The NLA should partner with the Institute for Nonprofit News, an organization that trains fledgling news organizations in professional, organizational, and business development, to recruit new editors to shape the future op-ed innovations. They could also work with the OpEd Project and with API, whose "Reimagining Opinion Journalism" summit in 2019 convened opinion editors to discuss innovations and best practices. News organizations will benefit from these investments: "If you put more resources into helping people themselves feel heard in a local opinion section, that process would teach you how to better reflect people in your reporting or would give you possibilities for hiring" (Loker, personal communication, June 29, 2020).

5.3 The Importance of Studying Local News

Political scientists and economists should pay closer attention to the steep decline in local news. The crisis facing this crucial mechanism of democratic accountability should worry not only political communication researchers, but also scholars of state, federal, and local government, policymaking, political behavior, and political psychology. While local news has its flaws, particularly when its coverage is tilted towards elites or disconnected from the community it serves (Usher 2019), it remains a powerful force for ensuring effective state and local governance (Snyder and Stromberg 2010) and strengthening cross-cutting community-based identities (Kaniss 1991). A narrow focus on the effects of partisan media or social media may obscure the role these media play in displacing or replacing local news in Americans' news diets. The subtraction of legacy outlets from the media marketplace is as relevant in understanding political communication today as the addition of new technologies and firms into the marketplace (Darr et al. 2018), and theories of the political effects of media change that ignore this fact are incomplete.

Surveys such as the General Social Survey (GSS), American National Election Studies (ANES), and Cooperative Congressional Election Study (CCES) should ask about the local or national focus of respondents' media use. Pew's local media use battery (Shearer 2020), or questions about specific sources respondents use (Dilliplane, Goldman, and Mutz 2013), would be welcome additions to these national surveys and should replace questions that only ask about medium without noting national or local focus. Adding these questions would provide scholars with publication opportunities and help us learn more about these crucial dynamics.

Finally, we highly recommend that scholars partner with local news organizations to test hypotheses about editorial decisions and civic outcomes, following the example of the Center for Media Engagement at the University of Texas, Austin, which helped fund this research. At every step of this project, the editors at *The Desert Sun* were enthusiastic and dedicated to helping us. Professional associations and philanthropists should encourage editors to try new approaches and could actively pair them with scholars who can help design interventions to test and assess editors' creative ideas for retaining readers and staying in business.

5.4 The Future of Local News and Opinion

If local newspapers are to survive, they need to collaborate with philanthropists and nonprofits, attract audiences with locally relevant information, and rally their community behind their product. The journalism industry is undoubtedly shifting away from local ownership and place-based reporting (Usher 2019). Whether or not that constitutes a "crisis" (see Zelizer 2015), it is imperative that local news organizations find cost-effective ways to deliver information that serves the critical information needs of their communities and readers (Friedland et al. 2012).

In July 2020, the hedge fund Chatham Asset Management purchased McClatchy, the nation's second-largest newspaper publisher (Atkinson 2020). McClatchy is an opinion page innovator, with a centralized operation across its thirty newspapers distributing best practices and prioritizing state and local issues (Nelson 2019). If the recent history of hedge fund newspaper ownership is any indication (Abernathy 2018), its opinion pages may now be in jeopardy.

In an age of national media saturation, local newspapers do not need to amplify the partisan arguments in Washington. Newspapers should open the door to local writers and present those perspectives on community issues. Loker agreed that a local focus could help newspapers: "If your organizational goals involve building an informed community and building subscribers locally ... putting more resources toward local opinions and fewer towards national makes sense" (Loker, personal communication, June 29, 2020).

July's local-only opinion page did not dislodge elite dominance on the opinion page. Local newspapers may be ill-equipped to tackle racial and gender disparities as they lose readers, revenues, and resources. The hedge fund and chain ownership groups that control many of America's newspapers are unlikely to address inequality on their opinion pages unless persuaded or pressured. Philanthropists and professional associations could help by funding and advancing initiatives that address racial, ethnic, and gender disparities in newsrooms, with a focus on opinion writing. Instead, the NLA, the largest professional organization for news editors, cancelled its forty-year-old diversity census in 2020 in order to retool its measurements (Edmonds 2020). Either way, they should be supported by journalism stakeholders, in addition to the $300,000 already supplied by Democracy Fund (Scire 2020).

Local opinion pages are particularly valuable during a crisis such as the COVID-19 pandemic, when newspapers are facing a grave economic threat. Many public health experts are engaging with the public on social media outlets such as Twitter (Warzel 2020), but op-eds published by trusted media, such as local newspapers, could make a greater impact on attitudes and behaviors (Coppock et al. 2018; Guess et al. 2018; King, Schneer, and White 2017; Miller and Krosnick 2000; Ciofalo and Traverso 1994). National news divides people by party, as we showed in Section 4. Public health information rife with partisan cues could polarize mask-wearing and other behaviors: in June 2020, for example, 76 percent of Democrats reported wearing masks in stores, compared to only 53 percent of Republicans (Igielnik 2020).

The salience of location as a group identity, which local media may strengthen, should reveal shared interests with other group members during threatening times (Mason 2018; Gay, Hochschild, and White 2016; Kaniss 1991). Group identity is arguably central to understanding American politics, but is rarely studied in relation to one's community, with some exceptions (Hopkins 2018; Cramer 2016; Wong 2010). The salience of community group identity, like other identities, may depend on current events and elite and media cues, placing added importance on the locality of local media (Mason 2018; Hoffman and Eveland 2010; Zaller 1992).

The COVID-19 pandemic of 2020/21 should make community-based group identity highly salient. The threat is directly tied to the virus' spread in one's community, and public health recommendations such as social distancing, wearing masks in public places, and washing hands depend on the cooperation and diligence of one's neighbors. Connectedness with other members of the community is an essential attitude at a time when everyone is relying on one another to follow public health recommendations in unison. Local media may strengthen these bonds and bolster important public health messages instead of fomenting division as national news does (Levendusky and Malhotra 2016; Kaniss 1991).

Local newspapers are uniquely positioned to unite communities around shared local identities, cultivated and emphasized through a distinctive home style, and provide a civil and regulated forum for debating solutions to local problems. In Palm Springs, those local issues were architectural restoration, traffic patterns, and environmental conservation. The issues will differ across communities, but a localized opinion page is more beneficial for newspapers and citizens than letters and op-eds speckled with national political vitriol. When national politics was removed from *The Desert Sun*, the space filled with state and local concerns, and afterwards people did not feel so far apart from one another. In Makinen's words, if we want to help local newspapers continue to make American democracy work better in spite of the existential crises they face today, "let's talk about home."

6 References

Abadie, A. (2005). "Semiparametric Difference-in-Differences Estimators." *Review of Economic Studies* 72(1): 1–19.

Abernathy, P.M. (2018). "The Expanding News Desert." Center for Innovation and Sustainability in Local Media, School of Media and Journalism, University of North Carolina at Chapel Hill.

Abernathy, P.M. (2020). "News Deserts and Ghost Newspapers: Will Local News Survive?" *A Report Published by the Center for Innovation and Sustainability* in Local Media, Chapel Hill, NC: University of North Carolina Press, www.usnewsdeserts.com/wpcontent/uploads/2020/06/2020_News_Deserts_and_Ghost_Newspapers.pdf.

Abramson, J.B., Arterton, F.C., and Orren, G.R. (1988). *The Electronic Commonwealth.* New York: Basic Books.

Achorn, E. (May 3, 2020). "Edward Achorn: A Personal Note to Readers." *Providence Journal*, www.providencejournal.com/opinion/20200503/edward-achorn-personal-note-to-readers.

Ackerman, E., Ambar, S., Amis, M., Applebaum, A., Arana, M., Atwood, M., . . . and Zakaria, F. (July 7, 2020). "A Letter on Justice and Open Debate." *Harper's Magazine*, https://harpers.org/a-letter-on-justice-and-open-debate/.

Allison, P. (2009). *Fixed Effects Regression Models* (Vol. 160). Thousand Oaks: SAGE.

Arceneaux, K. and Johnson, M. (2013). *Changing Minds or Changing Channels? Partisan news in an age of choice.* Chicago, IL: University of Chicago Press.

Arceneaux, K., Dunaway, J., Johnson, M., and Vander Wielen, R.J. (2020). "Strategic Candidate Entry and Congressional Elections in the Era of Fox News." *American Journal of Political Science*, 64(2), 398–415.

Archer, A. and Clinton, J. (2018). "Changing Owners, Changing Content: Does Who Owns the News Matter for the News?" *Political Communication*, 35(3), 353–70.

Armour-Jones, S. (2019). "Journalism Grantmaking: New Funding, Models and Partnerships to Sustain and Grow the Field." *A report published by Media Impact Funders*, Philadelphia, PA.

Arnold, R.D. (2004). *Congress, the Press, and Political Accountability.* Princeton, NJ: Princeton University Press.

ASNE. (2017). "AOJ-ASNE Merger," https://members.newsleaders.org/aoj-asne-merger.

Atkinson, C. (July 14, 2020). "Hedge Funds Scoop Up Local Newspapers Withering Under COVID-19 Cuts." NBCnews.com, www.nbcnews.com/business/business-news/hedge-funds-scoop-local-newspapers-withering-under-covid-19-cuts-n1233800.

Austin, D. and Bronat, D. (July 15, 2019). "Las Vegas or Palm Springs?" *Desert Sun* [Palm Springs, CA], p. 9A. Op-Ed.

Bakal, T. (July 15, 2019). "What Crew Wouldn't Want to Work Here?" *Desert Sun* [Palm Springs, CA], p. 9A. Op-Ed.

Baker, C. (2002). *Media, Markets, and Democracy, Communication, Society, and Politics*. Cambridge: Cambridge University Press.

Baker, G. (June 26, 2019). "NHL Seattle Chooses Palm Springs as Site for New AHL Farm Team." *The Seattle Times*, www.seattletimes.com/sports/hockey/nhl-seattle-chooses-palm-springs-as-site-for-new-ahl-farm-team/.

Baldassarri, D. and Gelman, A. (2008). "Partisans without Constraint: Political Polarization and Trends in American Public Opinion." *American Journal of Sociology*, 114(2): 408–46.

Barabas, J. and Jerit, J. (2009). "Estimating the Causal Effects of Media Coverage on Policy-Specific Knowledge." *American Journal of Political Science*, 53(1), 73–89.

Barabas, J., Jerit, J., Pollock, W., and Rainey, C. (2014). "The Question (s) of Political Knowledge." *American Political Science Review*, 840–55.

Bennett, W.L. (1990). "Toward a Theory of Press-State Relations." *Journal of Communication* 40(2): 103–25.

Benton, J. (May 12, 2020). "In Rhode Island, the State's Largest Daily no Longer Has Any Opinions of Its Own." NiemanLab, www.niemanlab.org/2020/05/in-rhode-island-the-states-largest-daily-no-longer-has-any-opinions-of-its-own/.

Bimber, B. (2003). *Information and American Democracy: Technology in the Evolution of Political Power*. New York: Cambridge University Press.

Blumberg, M. (July 30, 2019). "PS Unified Curriculum Spotlights Agua Caliente." *Desert Sun* [Palm Springs, CA], p. 13A. Op-Ed.

Branton, R.P. and Dunaway, J. (2009). "Slanted Newspaper Coverage of Immigration: The Importance of Economics and Geography." *Policy Studies Journal*, 37(2), 257–73.

Cain, B., Ferejohn, J., and Fiorina, M. (1987). *The Personal Vote: Constituency Service and Electoral Independence*. Cambridge, MA: Harvard University Press.

Cal State. (2020). "Introduction." The California State University., https://tinyurl.com/y6232p8a.

CALmatters,.(2020). "Dan Walters." Calmatters.org, https://calmatters.org/author/dan-walters/.

Campante, F. and Do, Q.-A. (2014). "Isolated Capital Cities, Accountability and Corruption: Evidence from U.S. States." *American Economic Review,* 104, 2456–81.

Campbell, J.E., Alford, J.R., and Henry, K. (1984). "Television Markets and Congressional Elections." *Legislative Studies Quarterly,* 665–78.

Canon, G. [@GabrielleCanon]. (April 24, 2020). [Tweet]. Twitter, https://twit ter.com/GabrielleCanon/status/1253844698310930433.

Card, D. and Kreuger A.B. (1993). "Minimum Wages and Employment: A Case Study of the Fast Food Industry in New Jersey and Pennsylvania." NBER Working Paper #4509.

Ciofalo, A. and Traverso, K. (1994). "Does the Op-Ed Page Have a Chance to Become a Public Forum?" *Newspaper Research Journal,* 15(4), 51–63.

City of Palm Springs. (2020). "City Profile," https://tinyurl.com/y5xn7yh3.

Clapp, R. (June 27, 2019). "The CV Link Lives." *Desert Sun* [Palm Springs, CA], p. 15A. Op-Ed.

Clifford, S. and Jerit, J. (2016). "Cheating on Political Knowledge Questions in Online Surveys: An Assessment of the Problem and Solutions." *Public Opinion Quarterly,* 80(4), 858–87.

Cohen, J. (2010). *Going Local: Presidential Leadership in the Post-Broadcast Age.* New York: Cambridge University Press.

Confessore, N. and Yourish, K. (March 15, 2016). "$2 Billion Worth of Free Media for Donald Trump." *New York Times,* www.nytimes.com/2016/03/16/ upshot/measuring-donald-trumps-mammoth-advantage-in-free-media.html.

Cook, T.D. and Campbell, D.T. (1979). *Quasi-Experimentation: Design and Analysis Issues for Field Settings.*New York: Houghton-Mifflin.

Cook, T.E. (1989). *Making Laws and Making News: Media Strategies in the U.S. House of Representatives.* Washington, DC: Brookings Institute.

Coppock, A., Ekins, E., and Kirby, D. (2018). "The Long-Lasting Effects of Newspaper Op-Eds on Public Opinion." *Quarterly Journal of Political Science,* 13(1), 59–87.

CVAG. (2015). "Top CVAG News," www.cvag.org/.

CVAG. (2016). "Welcome to the CV Link Project Information Page," www .coachellavalleylink.com/.

Darr, J. (2018). "Reports from the Field: Earned Local Media in Presidential Campaigns." *Presidential Studies Quarterly,* 48(2): 225–47.

Darr, J. and Dunaway, J. (2018). "Resurgent Mass Partisanship Revisited: The Role of Media Choice in Clarifying Elite Ideology." *American Politics Research,* 46(6): 943–70.

Darr, J., Hitt, M., and Dunaway, J. (2018). "Newspaper Closures Polarize Voting Behavior." *Journal of Communication,* 68(6): 1007–28.

Davis, N.T. (2018). "Identity Sorting and Political Compromise." *American Politics Research*, 47(2): 391–414.

Davis, N.T. and Dunaway, J.L. (2016). "Party Polarization, Media Choice, and Mass Partisan-Ideological Sorting." *Public Opinion Quarterly*, 80(S1): 272–97.

Davis, N.T. and Hitt, M.P. (2017). "Winning, Losing, and the Dynamics of External Political Efficacy." *International Journal of Public Opinion Research*, 29(4): 676–89.

Davis, N.T. and Mason, L. (2016). "Sorting and the Split-Ticket: Evidence from Presidential and Subpresidential Elections." *Political Behavior*, 38: 337–54.

Davis, R. (1999). *The Web of Politics: The Internet's Impact on the American Political System*. New York: Oxford University Press.

DellaVigna, S. and Kaplan, E. (2007). "The Fox News Effect: Media Bias and Voting." *Quarterly Journal of Economics*, 122(3): 1187–234.

Delli Carpini, M.X. and Keeter, S. (1997). *What Americans Know About Politics and Why it Matters*. New Haven, CT: Yale University Press.

Delli Carpini, M.X., Keeter, S., and Kennamer, J.D. (1994). "Effects of the News Media Environment on Citizen Knowledge of State Politics and Government." *Journalism Quarterly*, 71(2): 443–56.

Desert Sun. (September 30, 2016). "Hillary Clinton the Right Choice in Historic Election." *Desert Sun* [Palm Springs, CA], p. 13A. Editorial.

Desert Sun. (June 13, 2019). "Indian Wells, La Quinta Should Cooperate on Fix." *Desert Sun* [Palm Springs, CA], p. 13A. Editorial.

Desert Sun. (July 1, 2019). "Nestle Controversy Another Case of 'Hurry Up and Wait.'" *Desert Sun* [Palm Springs, CA], p. 13A. Editorial.

Desert Sun. (July 7, 2019). "PS Council, Take Time to Strike Best 1090 Deal with Grit Development." *Desert Sun* [Palm Springs, CA], p. A30. Editorial.

Dion, E. (February 29, 2020). "Projo People: Edward Achorn, the Man Behind the Editorial Pages." *Providence Journal*, www.providencejournal.com/news/20200229/projo-people-edward-achorn-man-behind-editorial-pages.

Doctor, K. (February 17, 2015). "What Are They Thinking? CALmatters Wants to Shake Up California Statehouse." Politico, www.politico.com/media/story/2015/02/what-are-they-thinking-calmatters-wants-to-shake-up-california-statehouse-003481.

Dunaway, J. (2008). "Markets, Ownership, and the Quality of Campaign News Coverage." *Journal of Politics*, 70(4): 1193–202.

Dunaway, J. (2011). "Institutional Effects on the Information Quality of Campaign News." *Journalism Studies*, 12(1): 27–44.

Dunaway, J. (2013). "Media Ownership and Story Tone in Campaign News." *American Politics Research*, 41(1): 24–53.

Dunaway, J. and Lawrence, R.G. (2015). "What Predicts the Game Frame? Media Ownership, Electoral Context, and Campaign News." *Political Communication*, 32(1): 43–60.

Edmonds, R. (August 5, 2019). "The GateHouse Takeover of Gannett Has Been Finalized." Poynter, www.poynter.org/reporting-editing/2019/the-gate house-takeover-of-gannett-has-been-finalized/.

Edmonds, R. (March 6, 2020). "Merged News Editors Group Is Canceling its 2020 Conference." Poynter, www.poynter.org/business-work/2020/merged-news-editors-group-is-canceling-its-2020-conference/.

Enda, J. (October 8, 2013). "In Print, Newspapers Cut Opinion." Pew Research Center, www.pewresearch.org/fact-tank/2013/10/08/in-print-newspapers-cut-opinion/.

Eshbaugh-Soha, M. (2010). "The Tone of Local Presidential News Coverage." *Political Communication*, 27(2): 121–40.

Fenno, R.F. (1978). *Home Style: Representatives in Their Districts*. Boston, MA: Little, Brown.

Ferrier, M., Sinha, G., and Outrich, M. (2016). "Media Deserts: Monitoring the Changing Media Ecosystem. In *The Communication Crisis in America, and How to Fix It* (pp. 215–32). New York: Palgrave Macmillan.

Festa, D. (July 4, 2019). "Water Systems Fair Use of Cap-and-Trade Funds." *Desert Sun* [Palm Springs, CA], p. 17A. Op-Ed.

Fowler, E.F. (2020). "Strategy Over Substance and National in Focus?: Local Television Coverage of Politics and Policy in the United States." In *The Routledge Companion to Local Media and Journalism* (pp. 185–92). London: Routledge.

Frank, R. (April 8, 2020). "COVID-19 Drives Traffic to News Sites, but Will Publishers Benefit?" News Media Alliance, www.newsmediaalliance.org/covid-drives-traffic-to-news-but-will-publishers-benefit/.

Friedland, L., Napoli, P., Ognyanova, K., Weil, C., and Wilson, E. (2012). "Review of the Literature Regarding Critical Infomration Needs of the American Public." Submitted to the Federal Communications Commission, https://transition.fcc.gov/bureaus/ocbo/Final_Literature_Review.pdf.

Fry, E. (May 29, 2012). "It's 2012 Already: Why is Opinion Writing Still Mostly Male?" *Columbian Journalism Review*, news/its_2012_already_why_is_opinion.php",1,0,0>https://archives.cjr.org/behind_the_</int_i> news/its_2012_already_why_is_opinion.php.

Gans, H.J. (1979). *Deciding What's News: A Study of CBS Evening News, NBC Nightly News, Newsweek, and Time*. New York: Random House, Inc.

Gardner, J. and Sullivan, B. (1999). "The National Newspaper as a Tool for Educational Empowerment: Origins and Rationale." [monograph].

New York Times, https://archive.nytimes.com/www.nytimes.com/ref/col lege/faculty/coll_mono_gard.html.

Gates, G. and Ost, J. (2004). *The Gay & Lesbian Atlas*. Washington, DC: Urban Institute Press.

Gelman, A. and Loken, E. (2014). "The Statistical Crisis in Science." *American Scientist*, 102: 460–65.

Gentzkow, M. and Shapiro, J.M. (2010). "What Drives Media Slant? Evidence from U.S. Daily Newspapers." *Econometrica: Journal of the Econometric Society*, 78, 35–71.

Gentzkow, M., Shapiro, J.M., and Sinkinson, M. (2011). "The Effect of Newspaper Entry and Exit on Electoral Politics." *American Economic Review*, 101(7): 2980–3018.

Gerber, E. and Hopkins, D. (2011). "When Mayors Matter: Estimating the Impact of Mayoral Partisanship on City Policy." *American Journal of Political Science*, 55(2): 326–39.

Gerber, A., Karlan, D., and Bergan, D. (2009). "Does the Media Matter? A Field Experiment Measuring the Effect of Newspapers on Voting Behavior and Political Opinions." *American Economic Journal: Applied Economics*, 1(2): 35–52.

Giorgis, H. (July 13, 2020). "A Deeply Provincial View of Free Speech." The Atlantic, www.theatlantic.com/culture/archive/2020/07/harpers-letter-free-speech/614080/.

Goldenberg, E. and Traugott,M. (1980). "Congressional Campaign Effects on Candidate Recognition and Evaluation." *Political Behavior*, 2(1): 61–90.

Gramlich, J. (2019). "Q&Q: What Pew Research Center's New Survey Says About Local News in the U.S.", www.pewresearch.org/fact-tank/2019/03/26/qa-what-pew-research-centers-new-survey-says-about-local-news-in-the-u-s/.

Gray, A. (2019). "California, It's Time to Recognize that Hydro-Power is 'Green.'" *Desert Sun* [Palm Springs, CA], p.13A. Op-Ed.

Grine, G. (July 25, 2019). "Enough, Road Warriors." *Desert Sun* [Palm Springs, CA], p. 13A. Op-Ed.

Guess, A., Nyhan, B., and Reifler, J. (2018). "All Media Trust is Local? Findings from the 2018 Poynter Media Trust Survey", www-personal.umich.edu/~bnyhan/media-trust-report-2018.pdf.

Hart, R.P. (2018). *Civic Hope: How Ordinary Americans Keep Democracy Alive*. Cambridge, MA: Cambridge University Press.

Hamilton, J.T. (2004). *All the News That's Fit to Sell: How the Market Transforms Information into News*. Princeton, NJ: Princeton University Press.

Hare, K. (2020). "The Coronavirus Has Closed More Than 25 Local Newsrooms." Poynter Institute, www.poynter.org/locally/2020/the-corona virus-has-closed-more-than-25-local-newsrooms-across-america-and-count ing/.

Hare, K. and Laforme, R. (April 24, 2020). "After Coronavirus Furloughs, Gannett Newspapers Lay Off Journalists Around the Country." Poynter, www.poynter.org/business-work/2020/after-coronavirus-furloughs-gannett-newspapers-lay-off-journalists-around-the-country/.

Hayes, D. and Lawless, J. (2015). "As Local News Goes, So Goes Citizen Engagement: Media, Knowledge, and Participation in U.S. House Elections." *Journal of Politics*, 77: 447–62.

Hayes, D. and Lawless, J. (2018). "The Decline of Local News and Its Effects: New Evidence from Longitudinal Data." *Journal of Politics*, 80(1): 332–6.

Haynes, D. (October 30, 2019). "Why the Milwaukee Journal Sentinel Replaced Opinion Content with Solutions Journalism." American Press Institute, www.americanpressinstitute.org/publications/reports/strategy-stud ies/why-the-milwaukee-journal-sentinel-replaced-opinion-content-with-solutions-journalism/.

Hindman, M. (2009). *The Myth of Digital Democracy*. Princeton, NJ: Princeton University Press.

Hindman, M. (2011). "Less of the Same: The Lack of Local News on the Internet." Report for the Federal Communications Commission, https://apps.fcc.gov/edocspublic/attachmatch/DOC-307476A1.pdf.

Hindman, M. (2014). "Stickier News: What Newspapers Don't Know About Web Traffic Has Hurt Them Badly but There is a Better Way." Shorenstein Center, Harvard Kennedy School, https://shorensteincenter.org/stickier-news-matthew-hindman/.

Hitt, M.P., Saunders, K.L., and Scott, K.M. (2019). "Justice Speaks, but Who's Listening? Mass Public Awareness of US Supreme Court Cases." *Journal of Law and Courts*, 7(1): 29–52.

Hobart, G.D. (July 28, 2019). "Sea of Cortez is Best, Realistic Solution." *Desert Sun* [Palm Springs, CA], p. 25A. Op-Ed.

Hoffman, L. and Eveland, W. (2010). "Assessing Causality in the Relationship between Community Attachment and Local News Media Use." *Mass Communication and Society*, 13(2): 174–95.

Hood, L. (2007). "Radio Reverb: The Impact of 'Local' News Reimported to Its Own Community." *Journal of Broadcasting & Electronic Media*, 51(1): 1–19.

Hopkins, D.J. (2018). *The Increasingly United States: How and Why American Political Behavior Nationalized*. Chicago, IL: University of Chicago Press.

Igielnik, R. (2020). "Most Americans Say They Regularly Wore A Mask in Stores in the Past Month; Fewer See Others Doing It." Pew Research Center, www.pewresearch.org/fact-tank/2020/06/23/most-americans-say-they-regularly-wore-a-mask-in-stores-in-the-past-month-fewer-see-others-doing-it/.

Innis, H.A. (1951). *The Bias of Communication*. Toronto: University of Toronto Press.

Institute for Nonprofit News. (2020). "The State of Nonprofit News: Entering a Crisis Year With Growing Audiences and Steady Finances", https://inn.org/innindex/.

Irfan, U. (November 5, 2019). "Trump's Fight with California Over Vehicle Emissions Rules Has Divided Automakers." Vox, httwww.vox.com/policy-and-politics/2019/11/5/20942457/california-trump-fuel-economy-auto-industry#:~:text=Trump%E2%80%99s%20fight%20with%20California%20over%20vehicle%20emissions%20rules,By%20Umair%20Irfan%20Nov%205%2C%202019%2C%203%3A30pm%20EST.

Iyengar S. and Krupenkin M. (2018). "Partisanship as Social Identity: Implications for the Study of Party Polarization." *The Forum* 16(1): 23–45.

Iyengar, S., Lelkes, Y., Levendusky, M., Malhotra, N., and Westwood, S. J. (2019). "The Origins and Consequences of Affective Polarization in the United States." *Annual Review of Political Science*, 22: 129–46.

Iyengar, S., Sood, G., and Lelkes, Y. (2012). "Affect, Not Ideology a Social Identity Perspective on Polarization." *Public Opinion Quarterly*, 76(3): 405–31.

Jacobs, R. and Townsley, E. (2011). *The Space of Opinion: Media Intellectuals and the Public Sphere*. New York: Oxford University Press.

Jacobson, G. (2013). *The Politics of Congressional Elections*, 8th ed. Harlow: Pearson.

Jennings, J. and Rubado, M. (2019). "Newspaper Decline and the Effect on Local Government Coverage." *A Report published by the Annette Strauss Institute for Civic Life*, Austin, TX: University of Texas at Austin.

Jimenez, R. (July 5, 2019). "Agricultural Housing Bill Would Help Fieldworkers." *Desert Sun* [Palm Springs, CA], p. 15A. Op-Ed.

Johns, G. (June 30, 2019). "*Include Town & Country Center in Talks.*" *Desert Sun* [Palm Springs, CA], p. 31A. Op-Ed.

Johns, G. (July 8, 2019). Palm Springs Preservation Foundation, http://pspreservationfoundation.org/tcc.html.

Johnson, H. and Sanchez, S. (2019). "Just the Facts: Immigrants in California." Public Policy Institute of California, www.ppic.org/publication/immigrants-in-california/.

Joyce, P. (1990). "Our Commentary Page is a Marketplace for ideas." *The Masthead*, 42.

Kahn, K.F. and Kenney, P.J. (2002). "The Slant of the News: How Editorial Endorsements Influence Campaign Coverage and Citizens' Views of Candidates." *American Political Science Review*, 96(2): 381–94.

Kam, C. and Zechmeister, E. (2013). "Name Recognition and Candidate Support." *American Journal of Political Science*, 57(4), 971–86.

Kaniss, P. (1991). *Making Local News*. Chicago, IL: University of Chicago Press.

Kaplan, M., Goldstein, K., and Hale, M. (2005). *Local News Coverage of the 2004 Campaigns*. Los Angeles, CA: USC Annenberg School and University of Wisconsin.

Kernell, S. (2006). *Going Public: New Strategies of Presidential Leadership*. Washington, DC: Cq Press.

Kinder, D. and Kalmoe, N. (2017). *Neither Liberal nor Conservative: Ideological Innocence in the American Public*. Chicago, IL: University of Chicago Press.

King, G. (1991). "On Political Methodology." *Political Analysis*, 2: 1–30.

King, G., Schneer, B., and White, A. (2017). "How the News Media Activate Public Expression and Influence National Agendas." *Science*, 358(6364): 776–80.

Klar, S., Krupnikov, Y., and Ryan, J. B. (2018). "Affective Polarization or Partisan Disdain? Untangling a Dislike for the Opposing Party from a Dislike of Partisanship." *Public Opinion Quarterly*, 82(2): 379–90.

Knight Foundation. (2019). State of Public Trust in Local News. Published Oct 20, 2019, https://tinyurl.com/y469yeyl.

Kujala, J. (2020). "Donors, Primary Elections, and Polarization in the United States." *American Journal of Political Science*, 64(3): 587–602.

Ladd, J.M. and Lenz, G.S. (2009). "Exploiting a Rare Communication Shift to Document the Persuasive Power of the News Media." *American Journal of Political Science*, 53(2): 394–410.

Lattig, J. (July 23, 2019). "Agenda Item 4.A – Proposed Grit Development LLC/Section 1090 Settlement." Palm Springs Preservation Foundation, http://pspreservationfoundation.org/tcc.html.

Layman, G. and Carsey, T. (2002). "Party Polarization and Party Structuring of Policy Attitudes: A Comparison of Three NES Panel Studies." *Political Behavior*, 24(3): 199–236.

Lee, C. (July 4, 2019). "A Vision of Endless Traffic." *Desert Sun* [Palm Springs, CA], p. 17A. Op-Ed.

Lelkes, Y., Sood, G., and Iyengar, S. (2017). "The Hostile Audience: The Efiect of Access to Broadband Internet on Partisan Afiect." *American Journal of Political Science*, 61: 5–20.

Levendusky, M. (2009). *The Partisan Sort: How Liberals became Democrats and Conservatives became Republicans*. Chicago, IL: University of Chicago Press.

Levendusky, M. and Malhotra, N. (2015). "(Mis)Perceptions of Partisan Polarization in the American Public." *Public Opinion Quarterly*.

Levendusky, M. and Malhotra, N. (2016). "Does Media Coverage of Partisan Polarization Afiect Political Attitudes?" *Political Communication*, 33, 283–301.

Levy, D. and Squire, P. (2000). "Television Markets and the Competitiveness of US House Elections." *Legislative Studies Quarterly*: 313–25.

Library of Congress. (2016). "U.S. Newspaper Directory, 1690—Present", http://chroniclingamerica.loc.gov/search/titles/.

Loker, K. (September 19, 2018). "Confusion About What's News and What's Opinion is a Big Problem, But Journalists Can Help Solve it." American Press Institute. www.americanpressinstitute.org/publications/confusion-about-whats-news-and-whats-opinion-is-a-big-problem-but-journalists-can-help-solve-it/.

Lueders, G. (July 21, 2019). "Safety is the Goal." *Desert Sun*, [Palm Springs, CA]. p. 25A. Op-Ed.

Lupia, A. (1994). "Shortcuts Versus Encyclopedias: Information and Voting Behavior in California Insurance Reform Elections." *American Political Science Review*, 88(1): 63–76.

Lyon, S. (July 19, 2019). "Skipping School Puts a Child's Future at Risk." *Desert Sun* [Palm Springs, CA], p. 11A. Op-Ed.

MacFarlane, M. (July 16, 2019). "Rules Keep Our Roads Safe." *Desert Sun* [Palm Springs, CA], p. 13A. Letter to the Editor.

Mahone, J., Wang, Q., Napoli, P., Weber, M., and McCollough, K. (2019). "Who's Producing Local Journalism? Assessing Journalistic Output Across Different Outlet Types." *A Report published by the DeWitt Wallace Center for Media & Democracy Sanford School of Public Policy*, Duke University, Durham, NC: Duke University Press.

Makinen, J. (2019a). "The Desert Sun Opinion Pages Are Taking a Summer Vacation from National Politics. You Can Help Us!" *Desert Sun* [Palm Springs, CA], p. 31A. Op-Ed.

Makinen, J. (2019b). "Desert Sun Adds Canon to Report from Sacramento." *Desert Sun* [Palm Springs, CA], p. 30A. Op-Ed.

Malacoff, R. (June 23, 2019). "Sunlight is Always Best." *Desert Sun* [Palm Springs, CA], p. 27A. Op-Ed.

Margolis, M., Resnick, D., and Wolfe, J. D. (1999). Party Competition on the Internet in the United States and Britain. *International Journal of Press/ Politics*, 4(4): 24–47.

Marksbury, J. (July 8, 2019). "Will the Arena Benefit Palm Springs?"*Desert Sun* [Palm Springs, CA], p. 9A. Op-Ed.

Marti, D. (July 22, 2019). "Researchers Lose Under UC Library's Adoption of Plan." *Desert Sun* [Palm Springs, CA], p. 9A. Op-Ed.

Martin, G.J. and McCrain, J. (2018). "The Political Consequences of Media Consolidation." Working paper.

Martin, G.J. and McCrain, J. (2019). "Local News and National Politics." *American Political Science Review*, 113(2): 372–84.

Marx, J. (December 7, 2016). "The Desert Voted Overwhelmingly for Clinton and Weed." *Desert Sun* [Palm Springs, CA], www.desertsun.com/story/ news/politics/elections/2016/12/07/desert-voted-overwhelmingly-clinton- and-weed/95111550/.

Mason, L. (2015). "'I Disrespectfully Agree': The Differential Effects of Partisan Sorting on Social and Issue Polarization." *American Journal of Political Science*, 59: 128–45.

Mason, L. (2016). "A Cross-Cutting Calm: How Social Sorting Drives Afiective Polarization." *Public Opinion Quarterly*, 80: 351–77.

Mason, L. (2018). *Uncivil Agreement: How Politics Became Our Identity*. Chicago, IL: University of Chicago Press.

Mayhew, D.R. (1974). *Congress: The Electoral Connection*. New Haven, CT: Yale University Press.

McCarthy, T. (July 18, 2019). "Trump Rally Crowd Chants 'Send Her Back' After President Attacks Illhan Omar." *The Guardian*, www.theguardian.com/ us-news/2019/jul/17/trump-rally-send-her-back-ilhan-omar.

McDermott, R. (2002). "Experimental Methods in Political Science." *Annual Review of Political Science*, 5: 31–61.

McKenzie, L. (April 26, 2018). "Florida State Cancels Bundled Journal Deal With Elsevier." *Inside Higher Ed*, www.insidehighered.com/quicktakes/ 2018/04/26/florida-state-cancels-bundled-journal-deal-elsevier.

McQuary, G. (June 23, 2019). "Say 'No' to Link Proposal." *Desert Sun* [Palm Springs, CA], p. 27A. Op-Ed.

Miller, J.M. and Krosnick, J.A. (2000). "News Media Impact on the Ingredients of Presidential Evaluations: Politically Knowledgeable Citizens Are Guided by a Trusted Source." *American Journal of Political Science*: 301–15.

Miringoff, J. (July 31, 2019). "The $100 Million Sidewalk Folly." *Desert Sun* [Palm Springs, CA], p. 13A.

Mitchell, H.J. and Flory, J. (July 12, 2019). "Let's Rethink Pricey Credit Issued in Medical Duress." *Desert Sun* [Palm Springs, CA], p. 11A. Op-Ed.

Molla, R. (May 7, 2019). "The Rise of Fear-Based Social Media Like Nextdoor, Citizen, and Now Amazon's Neighbors." Vox, www.vox.com/recode/2019/5/7/18528014fear-social-media-nextdoor-citizen-amazon-ring-neighbors.

Mondak, J. (1995). "Media Exposure and Political Discussion in U.S. Elections." *Journal of Politics*, 57(1): 62–85.

Mondak, J.J. (1995). "Newspapers and Political Awareness." *American Journal of Political Science*: 513–27.

Mondak, J. (1995). *Nothing to Read: Newspapers and Elections in a Social Experiment*. Ann Arbor: University of Michigan Press.

Morrison, M. (July 4, 2019). "'Refreshing' Limits?" *Desert Sun* [Palm Springs, CA]. p. 17A. Op-Ed.

Moskowitz, D. (2020). "Local News, Information, and the Nationalization of U.S. Elections." *American Political Science Review*, First View, https://doi.org/10.1017/S0003055420000829.

NAES (2000). "National Annenberg Election Survey." Annenberg Public Policy Center of the University of Pennsylvania, www.annenbergpublicpolicycenter.org/political-communication/naes/.

Napoli, P.M. (2002). *Audience Economics: Media Institutions and the Audience Marketplace*. New York: Columbia University Press.

Napoli, P.M. and Yan, M.Z. (2007). "Media Ownership Regulations and Local News Programming on Broadcast Television: An Empirical Analysis." *Journal of Broadcasting & Electronic Media*, 51(1): 39–57.

Napoli, P.M., Stonbely, S., McCollough, K., and Renninger, B. (2017). "Local Journalism and the Information Needs of Local Communities: Toward a Scalable Assessment Approach." *Journalism Practice*, 11(4): 373–95.

Nelson, C.M. (October 30, 2019). "Why McClatchy Opinion Sections Are Speaking Boldly." American Press Institute, www.americanpressinstitute.org/publications/reports/strategy-studies/why-mcclatchy-opinion-sections-are-speaking-boldly/.

Neustadt, R.E. (1980). *Presidential Power and the Modern Presidents: The Politics of Leadership from Roosevelt to Reagan*. New York: Simon & Schuster.

Newell, S. and Metz, S. (January 24, 2019). "Palm Springs Mayor Rob Moon Won't Run in 2019, Says Council is Moving 'So Far to the Left'." *Desert Sun* [Palm Springs, CA], www.desertsun.com/story/news/local/2019/01/24/palm-springs-mayor-rob-moon-wont-run-2019/2668708002/.

New York Times. (September 21, 1970). "Op. Ed. Page", www.nytimes.com/1970/09/21/archives/op-ed-page.html.

Nosek, B.A., Alter, G., and Banks,G.C. et al. (2015). "Promoting an Open Research Culture." *Science*, 348(6242): 1422–5.

Nunez, F. (July 3, 2019). "State Must Stop Diverting Cap-and-Trade Revenue." *Desert Sun* [Palm Springs, CA], p. 15A. Op-Ed.

Nyhan, B. and Reifler, J. (2010). "When Corrections Fail: The Persistence of Political Misperceptions." *Political Behavior*, 32(2): 303–30.

OpEd Project. (May 28, 2012). "The Byline Survey Report, 2012: Who Narrates the World?" The Byline Blog, https://theopedproject.wordpress.com/2012/05/28/.

OpEd Project. (2020). www.theopedproject.org/.

Padgett, J., Dunaway, J.L., and Darr, J.P. (2019). "As Seen on TV? How Gatekeeping Makes the US House Seem More Extreme." *Journal of Communication*, 69(6): 696–719.

Page, B. (1996). *Who Deliberates?: Mass Media in Modern Democracy.* Chicago, IL: University of Chicago Press.

Peterson, E. (2019). "Not Dead Yet: Political Learning from Newspapers in a Changing Media Landscape." *Political Behavior*: 1–23.

Peterson, E. (2020). "Paper Cuts: How Reporting Resources Affect Political News Coverage." In press, *American Journal of Political Science*.

Pew Research Center (March 26, 2019). "For Local News, Americans Embrace Digital but Still Want Strong Community Connection", www.journalism.org/2019/03/26/for-local-news-americans-embrace-digital-but-still-want-strong-community-connection/.

Pew Research Center. (June 25, 2019). "Local TV News Fact Sheet", www.journalism.org/fact-sheet/local-tv-news/.

Pew Research Center. (July 9, 2019). "Newspapers Fact Sheet", www.journalism.org/fact-sheet/newspapers/.

Pickard, V. (2019). *Democracy Without Journalism: Confronting the Misinformation Society.* Oxford: Oxford University Press.

Plazas, D. (October 30, 2019). "How the Tennessean's Opinion Section is Working to Combat Polarization." American Press Institute, www.americanpressinstitute.org/publications/reports/strategy-studies/how-the-tennesseans-opinion-section-is-working-to-combat-polarization/.

Pompeo, J. (February 5, 2020). "The Hedge Fund Vampire That Bleeds Newspapers Dry Now Has the Chicago Tribune by the Throat." Vanity Fair, www.vanityfair.com/news/2020/02/hedge-fund-vampire-alden-global-capital-that-bleeds-newspapers-dry-has-chicago-tribune-by-the-throat.

Prato, L. (1998). "In Local TV News We Trust, But Why?" *American Journalism Review*, 68.

Price, V. and Zaller, J. (1993). "Who Gets the News? Alternative Measures of News Reception and Their Implications for Research." *Public Opinion Quarterly*, 57(2): 133–64.

Prior, M. (2007). *Post-Broadcast Democracy*. New York: Cambridge University Press.

Quinn, G. (2020). "Do Gun Policy Specifics Matter? Hyper-Polarization and the Decline of Vote Splitting in Congress." *The Forum*, 18(2): 249–82.

Rivkin, M. (July 19, 2019). "Our Bighorn Sheep Are Summer Soldiers." *Desert Sun* [Palm Springs, CA], p. 11A. Op-Ed.

Robinson-Jacobs, K. (February 6, 2020). "This Architect of Classic Hollywood Gets His Own Star Turn." *Los Angeles Times*, www.latimes.com/business/real-estate/story/2020-02-06/architect-paul-williams-documentary.

Rosen, J. (1993). *Community Connectedness Passwords for Public Journalism: How to Create Journalism That Listens to Citizens and Reinvigorates Public Life*. St. Petersburg, FL: Poynter Institute for Media Studies.

Rosenberg, A. (May 9, 2020). "Alan Rosenberg: The End of an Era of Editorials." *Providence Journal*, www.providencejournal.com/news/20200509/alan-rosenberg-end-of-era-of-editorials.

Rosenfeld, S.S. (2000). "The Op-Ed Page: A Step to a Better Democracy." *Harvard International Journal of Press/Politics*, 5(3): 7–11.

Rubado, M.E. and Jennings, J.T. (2019). "Political Consequences of the Endangered Local Watchdog: Newspaper Decline and Mayoral Elections in the United States." *Urban Affairs Review*. 1078087419838058.

Rude, T. (July 13, 2019). "On Board for This 'Break.'" *Desert Sun* [Palm Springs, CA], p. 23A. Op-Ed.

Schaffner, B.F. (2006). "Local News Coverage and the Incumbency Advantage in the US House." *Legislative Studies Quarterly*, 31(4): 491–511.

Schaffner, B.F. and Sellers, P.J. (2003). "The Structural Determinants of Local Congressional News Coverage." *Political Communication*, 20(1): 41–57.

Schmidt, C. (July 10, 2019). "How CALmatters is Growing Out of Its Startup Stage." NiemanLab, www.niemanlab.org/2019/07/how-calmatters-is-growing-out-of-its-startup-stage/.

Schmidt, C. (September 18, 2019). "Nonprofit News Outlets Aren't Relying as Heavily on Foundations – but Journalism Philanthropy Continues to Grow." Nieman Lab, www.niemanlab.org/2019/09/nonprofit-news-outlets-arent-relying-as-heavily-on-foundations-but-journalism-philanthropy-continues-to-grow/.

Schulhofer-Wohl, S. and Garrido, M. (2013). "Do Newspapers Matter? Short-Run and Long-Run Evidence from the Closure of The Cincinnati Post." *Journal of Media Economics*, 26(2): 60–81.

Scire, S. (May 26, 2020). "A Window Into One Newsroom's Diversity Opens but an Industry-Wide Door Shuts (For Now)." NiemanLab, www.niemanlab.org/2020/05/a-,indow-into-one-newsrooms-diversity-opens-but-an-industry-wide-door-shuts-for-now/.

Seeger, M. (July 24, 2019). "Our Desert Offers Places to Recharge Your Soul." *Desert Sun* [Palm Springs, CA], p. 13A. Op-Ed.

Seldner, J. (1994). "Voice of the Privileged." *Nieman Reports*, 48(1): 89.

Semes, R. (June 13, 2019). "Thanks For the Break." *Desert Sun* [Palm Springs, CA], p. 13A. Op-Ed.

Shaker, L. (2009). "Citizens' Local Political Knowledge and the Role of Media Access." *Journalism & Mass Communication Quarterly*, 86(4): 809–26.

Shaker, L. (2014). "Dead Newspapers and Citizens' Civic Engagement." *Political Communication*, 31: 131–148.

Shipley, D. (2004). "And Now a Word from Op-Ed." *New York Times*. February 1, section 4, p. 11. www.nytimes.com/2004/02/01/opinion/and-now-a-word-from-op-ed.html.

Sides, J., Tesler, M., and Vavreck, L. (2018). "Hunting Where the Ducks Are: Activating Support for Donald Trump in the 2016 Republican Primary." *Journal of Elections, Public Opinion and Parties*, 28(2): 135–56.

Smith, B. (June 7, 2020). "Inside the Revolts Erupting in America's Big Newsrooms." *New York Times*, www.nytimes.com/2020/06/07/business/media/new-york-times-washington-post-protests.html.

Snyder, J. and Stromberg, D. (2010). "Press Coverage and Political Accountability." *Journal of Political Economy*, 118: 355–408.

Socolow, M.J. (2010). "A Profitable Public Sphere: the Creation of the New York Times Op-Ed Page." *Journalism & Mass Communication Quarterly*, 87(2): 281–96.

Sommer, B. and Maycroft, J.R. (2008). "Influencing Public Policy: An Analysis of Published Op-Eds by Academics." *Politics & Policy*, 36(4): 586–613.

Spencer, S. (June 13, 2019). "A 'Genius' Move." *Desert Sun* [Palm Springs, CA], p. 13A. Op-Ed.

Stroud, N.J. (2017). "Attention as a Valuable Resource." *Political Communication*, 34(3): 479–89.

Suiter, J. and Fletcher, R. (2020). "Polarization and Partisanship: Key Drivers of Distrust in Media Old and New?" *European Journal of Communication*, 35(5): 484–501.

Talmy, R. (July 9, 2019). "It's the Traffic Stupid.". *Desert Sun* [Palm Springs, CA], p. 13A. Letter to the Editor.

Tracy, M. (June 7, 2020). "James Bennet Resigns as New York Times Opinion Editor. *New York Times*, https://tinyurl.com/y5gzv5rz.

Trounstine, J. (2009). "All Politics is Local: The Reemergence of the Study of City Politics." *Perspectives on Politics*, 7(3): 611–18.

Trussler, M. (2018). "The Efiects of High Information Environments on the Incumbency Advantage and Partisan Voting." *Paper presented at the annual meeting of the Midwest Political Science Association*, Chicago, IL.

Trussler, M. 2020. "Get Information or Get in Formation: The Effects of High-Information Environments on Legislative Elections." *British Journal of Political Science*, First View: 1–21.

UC Newsroom. (September 10, 2019). "UC Campuses Top the 2020 US News & World Report Rankings." University of California, www.universityofcali fornia.edu/news/uc-campuses-top-2020-us-news-world-report-rankings.

UC Office of Scholarly Communication (2019). "Open Statement: Why UC Terminated Journal Negotiations With Elsevier." University of California, https://osc.universityofcalifornia.edu/2019/03/open-statement-why-uc-ter minated-journal-negotiations-with-elsevier/.

U.S. Census Bureau. (2019). "Quickfacts: Palm Springs City, California", www.census.gov/quickfacts/palmspringscitycalifornia.

Vasquez, F. and Eveslage, T. (1983). *Newspapers' Letters to the Editor as Reflections of Social Structure*. Distributed by ERIC Clearinghouse.

Vinson, D. (2003). *Local Media Coverage of Congress and Its Members: Through Local Eyes*. Cresskill, NJ: Hampton.

Visit Palm Springs. (2019). "About Palm Springs", www.visitpalmsprings.com/ about-palm-springs.

Wagner, M. and Collins, T. (2014). "Does Ownership Matter? The Case of Rupert Murdoch's Purchase of the *Wall Street Journal*." *Journalism Practice*, 8(6): 758–71.

Waldman, S. (2011). "Information Needs of Communities: The Changing Media Landscape in a Broadband Age." FCC, www.fcc.gov/infoneedsreport.

Warzel, C. (July 23, 2020). "They Want Your Attention. Don't Give It to Them." *New York Times*. Op-Ed, www.nytimes.com/2020/07/23/opinion/cancel-cul ture.html.

Whetstone, G. (July 1, 2019). "Traffic Safety Vital in the Desert." *Desert Sun* [Palm Springs, CA], p. 13A. Op-Ed.

Winet, R. and Winet, M. (June 13, 2019). "Vacation from National Politics." *Desert Sun* [Palm Springs, CA], p. 13A. Op-Ed.

Wirth, M. and Wollert, J. (1979). "Public Interest Programming: Taxation by Regulation." *Journal of Broadcasting*, 23(3): 319–30.

Wilson, S. (February 18, 2019). "In Palm Springs, the Nation's First All-LGBTQ City Council Tests the Modern Meaning of Diversity." *Washington Post*, www.washingtonpost.com/national/in-palm-springs-the-nations-first-all-lgbtq-city-council-tests-the-modern-meaning-of-diversity/ 2019/02/18/38f9b600-3074-11e98ad3-9a5b113ecd3c_story.html.

Wolf, N. (November 29, 1995). "Are Opinions Male?" *New Republic*: 20–6.

Wood, T. and Porter, E. (2019). "The Elusive Backfire Effect: Mass Attitudes' Steadfast Factual Adherence." *Political Behavior*, 41(1): 135–63.

Yaeger, T. (May 28, 2012). "The Byline Survey Report, 2012: Who Narrates the World?" The Byline Blog, https://theopedproject.wordpress.com/2012/05/ 28/the-byline-survey-2011/.

Yan, M. and Napoli, P. (2006). "Market Competition, Station Ownership, and Local Public Affairs Programming on Broadcast Television." *Journal of Communication*, 56(4): 795–812.

Yepello, V. (July 25, 2019). "CV Link is Our Future." *Desert Sun* [Palm Springs, CA], p. 13A. Op-Ed.

York, C. (2013). "Cultivating Political Incivility: Cable News, Network News, and Public Perceptions." *Electronic News*, 7: 107–25.

Acknowledgments

We thank several sources for their financial support for this research, including the D. Jensen Holliday and Kevin P. Reilly professorships from the Manship School of Mass Communication at LSU; Texas A&M University's College of Liberal Arts; and Talia Stroud and the Center for Media Engagement at the University of Texas at Austin. Caleb Snider and Krislyn Flores provided excellent research assistance. We thank attendees of the SSRC Workshop on News Coverage of US Elections and APSA 2020 for their comments, series editor Stuart Soroka for his stewardship throughout the process, and the anonymous reviewers for making this manuscript better with their insightful comments. Any errors or omissions are our own. We would particularly like to thank Julie Makinen and Al Franco of *The Desert Sun* for their idea, the hard work it took to make it a reality, and their enthusiastic cooperation with this project. We dedicate this book to the memory of Martin Johnson, whose enthusiastic support made this research possible and whose friendship, leadership, and scholarship are missed every day. Finally, we would like to thank our families for their support in getting this project finished in the middle of a pandemic. We couldn't have done it without you.

Cambridge Elements ≡

Elements in Politics and Communication

Stuart Soroka

University of Michigan

Stuart Soroka is the Michael W. Traugott Collegiate Professor of Communication and Media & Political Science, and research professor in the Center for Political Studies at the Institute for Social Research, University of Michigan. His research focuses on political communication, the sources and/or structure of public preferences for policy, and the relationships between public policy, public opinion, and mass media. His books include *Negativity in Democratic Politics* (2014) and *Degrees of Democracy* (with Christopher Wlezien, 2010), both with Cambridge University Press.

About the Series

Cambridge Elements in Politics and Communication publishes research focused on the intersection of media, technology, and politics. The series emphasizes forward-looking reviews of the field, path-breaking theoretical and methodological innovations, and the timely application of social-scientific theory and methods to current developments in politics and communication around the world.